"Támara Hill has produced a book worth reader. As such, it contains helpful and jump-start a long-overdue conversation regarding the often taboo subject of race and mental health in our country. What I admire most about this book, however, is Hill's hopefulness and her ability to convey empathy in a refreshing and insightful fashion."

—**Don Laird, NCC, LPC, DCC**, psychotherapist;
and founder of eTalkTherapy, LLC

"The Racial Trauma Handbook for Teens is a powerful book for Black and mixed-race teens, and for parents or guardians raising a Black or mixed-race child. The reflection activities and self-care strategies Támara Hill provides helps teens process racialized experiences and heal from racial trauma. It is heartbreaking that our children experience such trauma; however, this book will help guide them through these moments and develop confidence and self-love."

—**Kaii Marie Robertson**, restorative therapeutic yoga
instructor and wellness educator, and cofounder of
The Behavioral Health and Mind Body Economy

"This phenomenal handbook fills a crucial resource gap with its relevance and responsiveness to the needs of Black and multiracial teenagers. The content is clinically sound, culturally respectful, and developmentally appropriate. Teen readers will appreciate how the book offers clarity for complex emotions, and provides relatable examples along with activities that bring concepts to life. Bravo, Támara Hill! This handbook holds count-less keys to intergenerational wellness."

—**LaVerne Hanes Collins, PhD, LCMHC, LPC**,
counselor educator; diversity trainer; and owner/CEO of
New Seasons Counseling, Training and Consulting, LLC

"Infused with the heartfelt struggles of growing up as a multiethnic child, Támara Hill takes Black and mixed-race teens on a journey to explore their personal experiences with racism and intergenerational trauma, and models healthy, compassionate self-reflection tools and coping skills that empower teens to heal from the impacts of racial trauma in a positive way. A must-read for educators, as most trauma-informed teaching practices are viewed through a narrow lens that does NOT include race-based stress and trauma."

—**Lori Maldonado**, professional development coordinator
at www.simplek12.com, education technology trainer,
national conference speaker, and secondary science instructor

"Támara Hill has provided a powerful overview of a challenging and relevant topic. The insight and practical tools make this book a must-read! Resiliency, grit, mindfulness, post-traumatic growth, antifragility...it's all in here. When someone's personal experience fuels the passion for hard work and dedication to the community, you get a resource like this. This book will be on every contemporary therapist's shelf."

—**Anat Samid, LCSW**, emotional intelligence life coach
and psychotherapist

the *i* n s t a n t   h e l p
s o l u t i o n s   s e r i e s

Young people today need mental health resources more than ever. That's why New Harbinger created the **Instant Help Solutions Series** especially for teens. Written by leading psychologists, physicians, and professionals, these evidence-based self-help books offer practical tips and strategies for dealing with a variety of mental health issues and life challenges teens face, such as depression, anxiety, bullying, eating disorders, trauma, and self-esteem problems.

Studies have shown that young people who learn healthy coping skills early on are better able to navigate problems later in life. Engaging and easy-to-use, these books provide teens with the tools they need to thrive—at home, at school, and on into adulthood.

This series is part of the **New Harbinger Instant Help Books** imprint, founded by renowned child psychologist Lawrence Shapiro. For a complete list of books in this series, visit newharbinger.com.

THE
RACIAL TRAUMA
HANDBOOK
FOR TEENS

CBT Skills to Heal from the Personal & Intergenerational Trauma of Racism

TÁMARA HILL, LPC

Instant Help Books
An Imprint of New Harbinger Publications, Inc.

Publisher's Note

This publication is designed to provide accurate and authoritative information in regard to the subject matter covered. It is sold with the understanding that the publisher is not engaged in rendering psychological, financial, legal, or other professional services. If expert assistance or counseling is needed, the services of a competent professional should be sought.

INSTANT HELP, the Clock Logo, and NEW HARBINGER are trademarks of New Harbinger Publications, Inc.

New Harbinger Publications is an employee-owned company.

Copyright © 2023 by Támara Hill
Instant Help Books
An imprint of New Harbinger Publications, Inc.
5674 Shattuck Avenue
Oakland, CA 94609
www.newharbinger.com

Cover design by Amy Shoup; Acquired by Jennye Garibaldi; Edited by Karen Schader

Library of Congress Cataloging-in-Publication Data on file

Printed in the United States of America

25   24   23

10   9   8   7   6   5   4   3   2   1   First Printing

This book is dedicated to the mixed-race and Black individuals and families I have had the pleasure of crossing paths with. You have taught me a lot.

Contents

Foreword

Growing up as a Black boy in the United States, I have witnessed firsthand the hardships of living in an urban community where society doesn't always see your humanity; I was also one of few students of color in the classroom as I entered college. These experiences have all shaped my life in different ways. Understanding how race impacted my life and the lives of other minoritized communities led me to my career as a psychologist. My work providing therapy and doing research has focused on addressing the needs of youth and their families. This passion has resulted from (1) recognizing how racism and oppression in society impacts mental health and (2) a desire to reduce stigma around addressing mental health among Black youth and their families. More than ever, it is now time to confront these issues, given the continued racism within society and our communities.

Life can be challenging and stressful for teens—particularly for teens from diverse racial backgrounds. Some research notes that youth of color experience at least one incident of racial discrimination in their life, yet these youth or their parents do not commonly know how to cope with the mental health challenges associated with racism. In my work as a psychologist, I have encountered many teens and their parents who have been impacted by negative statements about their race or identity. While therapy is a great resource to help address racial stress or trauma, many people are not able to access therapy to address these concerns. Sometimes the inability to get therapy is due to financial reasons; other times, teens may not be ready to talk about these types of situations in therapy. Some parents may not recognize that therapy is the best approach to help their child.

The Racial Trauma Handbook for Teens can help you understand ways to think through situations you have experienced as a result of racial discrimination. It is an accessible self-help guide you can use to process and heal from experiences of racism that may lead to self-hate, hurt, anger, or sadness.

In Part 1 of this book, the author discusses racial trauma and how experiencing racism can impact you and your family. What we know from research on racism and racial stress is that not everyone will experience what is known as racial trauma. Scholars such as Robert Carter and Thema Bryant have discussed how single or repeated incidents of racism can impact each person differently. This book provides an opportunity for you to think about your experiences and to consider how other teens from your racial background may have had similar experiences.

Part 2 of the book offers options to help you heal and cope with stress related to racism. Although it can be difficult to know what to do after you have a negative racial encounter or experience racism, the Racial Trauma Handbook for Teens offers several strategies for you to consider. As a psychologist, I often tell my clients to create a list of things to do in stressful situations so that if one doesn't work for you in the moment, you can try another to help relieve your stress.

This book is a useful resource that provides practical activities on understanding racism and microaggressions, offers resources to help you understand how your body responds to racial stress, and helps you explore signs of trauma that results from racism and discrimination. Given the frequency of racism and discrimination, the *Racial Trauma Handbook for Teens* is so needed.

—Erlanger A. Turner, PhD
Associate Professor of Psychology in
the Graduate School of Education and
Psychology at Pepperdine University
and founder of Therapy for Black Kids

Introduction: Why We Need This Book

Growing up as a multiethnic child was difficult. I didn't always fit in with kids my own age, and I often preferred the loner lifestyle, perhaps partly because our neighborhood was predominately White, with one Black family down the street from my house. My racial heritage—Native American, Northern African, and Black—was never respected or appreciated because my community saw my family as being only Black.

Sadly, my own extended family struggled to learn about and appreciate the mixture of cultures in our blood. The fact that I chose to embrace my many cultures created what I felt was tension and rejection within my community and my family. Being raised differently set me apart quite a bit, and I felt the divide all throughout my childhood. Even attempts to connect with my own family—who are culturally different from each other in many ways—was difficult. Finding my racial identity came only after I went to college—a predominately White college in a rich neighborhood—and was forced by specific circumstances to embrace my racial identity. Learning about myself, my culture, and my family's racial trauma led me to develop a confidence and determination that would push me forward past any bullying, harassment, rejection, and racism I experienced.

After becoming a child and family therapist, I increasingly realized that I wasn't the only one experiencing the pain of rejection as a multiethnic Black person. I saw many kids and families in my office who reported being bullied at school, in the neighborhood, and in their broader communities because of their race. And I could feel exactly how frequent experiences of racism and discrimination—including racism that isn't easy to see in the moment—can cause you to doubt yourself and isolate, withdraw, and feel defeated. This newly strengthened insight about racism was a turning point for my career and my own personal growth. It's like I had to be awakened to the truth.

And while the trauma you may have experienced from racism may be considerable, you, too, could have a turning point. Maybe you feel singled out in your own family, community, or school. Maybe you feel hopeless or depressed because of who you are and how others may see you. In this book, I encourage you to feel confident about who you are.

Throughout this book I have used the terms "Black" and "mixed race" to discuss differences and similarities in these groups' experiences of racism. Whether you are Black or of mixed race, in order to grow from your own experiences, you must develop an accurate, authentic vision of yourself in the world—one that *isn't* influenced by all the unfair stereotypes and biases our society imposes.

Developing an accurate view of yourself may require that you work through painful thoughts, feelings, and beliefs about who you are as a person in a racist society. Doing this work will allow you to understand yourself for who *you are*—not who people *think* that you, or Black or mixed-race people, are—and to understand your family and your community in the same way. It will also help you ignore all the painful thoughts you have had about yourself as a Black or mixed-race person. Racism is something that every Black or mixed-race person will likely experience at some point in their lives. Since the beginning of slavery in the United States and elsewhere, Black people have been misjudged, silenced, and ignored, which has caused centuries of shame, doubt, and fear.

It's also true that racism today—after the era of slavery, and after the Jim Crow era, the period in which racism was encoded in law—isn't always obvious. Because of this, racism in today's world can feel a lot like intimidation and emotional abuse. For example, unfair beliefs or comments such as the ones below can make you feel bad about yourself and cause feelings of shame for a very long time:

- "Black kids are *raised* wrong."

- "Black kids are really *good* at basketball and rapping."

- "I don't want my son playing with kids from *that* neighborhood."

- "Biracial kids are always confused about who they are. They have no identity."

- "Is your hair as soft as it looks?"

These racist comments may not always be said out loud, but they can be deeply felt. One such form of racism is known as *microaggression*. Microaggressions are brief expressions, tones of voice, or comments and behaviors that are subtle, but inflict harm because of the way they reveal racist attitudes toward certain groups of people.

You might also encounter more severe and intentional kinds of racism. For example, you may hear your peers use the N-word on your school bus or in your school because they don't acknowledge the painful history associated with this word. You may also see someone blatantly mistreat or follow someone around in a public place because of the color of their skin. You may not be able to prove it, but you know something doesn't feel right to you.

Another form of racism that you may notice is *ambient racism*—the unfair treatment of Black or mixed-race people on the news or social media in a way that appears harmless but is deeply racist. For instance, you might hear a lot about Black people, in particular, receiving harsh treatment from the police or authorities. Seeing the ways that people who look like you or are part of your community can be mistreated—and how the people who mistreat them are often not held accountable—can cause you a lot of subtle stress you might not even realize you have. You might even hear about the unfair treatment of Black people on the news and feel the reports are not 100 percent truthful. For example, if someone on the news talks about the Black Lives Matter movement with a comment like "Black lives aren't the only ones that matter," that can be considered ambient racism. It completely misses the point that the Black Lives Matter movement is trying to get across to the world. Although it's not directed at you, hearing it still causes you harm.

And then there's the experience of *structural racism* in schools. Teachers who are teaching without an awareness of cultural differences and learning styles can show racism in how they teach, grade assignments, and respond to Black and mixed-race students. Research on the racial achievement gap—a gap between Black and White students who are graded differently because of their race—has shown that Black students are often graded lower than their White peers. It can be very frustrating to Black and mixed-race students to try their very best on assignments but only receive a B as a grade. Although structural racism may be difficult to prove, it doesn't mean it isn't truly happening to Black or mixed-race students.

Repeatedly experiencing racism—or seeing someone impacted by this kind of racism—can cause you to experience racial trauma. And if you continue to have these kinds of experiences of racism, or to see them affecting people you know, you can begin to experience stress, nightmares, poor sleep, sad moods, tearfulness, high anxiety, and shame. You might behave in ways that harm not only yourself but also the people around you, even if you don't mean to. In fact, maybe you've had the experience of caregivers or family members behaving angrily toward each other or toward you because of racist experiences they had that they couldn't actually address in the moment, or because of the stress of having to live in a society where you're told you're second-class.

This stress reflects the way that racial trauma can affect not just us as individuals but also our families across the generations. Intergenerational trauma can change the way your family interacts with each other. We'll talk about that too. Ultimately, racial trauma makes it hard for you to live the life that you, like everyone else, deserve to live: a life in which you feel safe and worthy as a person, and you can do the things you really want to do. This book is primarily about identifying your own racial trauma, and the trauma that has affected your family, and learning healthy coping skills to manage the negative thoughts you might be having—skills that will help you turn pain into self-care, growth, and strength. You will also be able to reflect on the beauty of your culture and who you are as a person as you learn new skills and new ways of thinking about racism.

What You'll Find in This Book

Part 1 of this book helps you define your individual and family experience with racism. You'll learn about the signs and symptoms of racial trauma and the widespread effects it can have in your life as a Black or mixed-race person. It is very important to explore your experience with racism so that you can understand exactly what emotions you're feeling and build skills to manage them. Anyone who's experienced racism will find that the messages our society gives us through the way others treat us come to permeate their own thoughts. That is, you may think things like *I wonder if anyone will ever like me*; *I feel like my family will never be able to be fully safe and happy*; *I wonder if things will ever change*; *I wonder if things would change if I weren't Black*. These inner voices are remnants of racism. The things they say are not the truth. Through conversations over the years with many Black and mixed-race people, I have learned how to silence the negative voices in my mind that can cause me to internalize shame and forget what it truly means to be a Black and multiethnic person, to know that I don't have to let those voices control what I do. If you learn to accept who you are—and appreciate who you are—you can heal from racial trauma.

If your family is struggling with racial trauma, it can be really isolating to see the ways they might be ignoring the problem. You may feel that certain people in your family seem not to care about your struggles with race. Maybe they just tell you to take it and move on. Maybe they don't want to acknowledge it exists at all. Feeling as though the people you love are ignoring what you're all going through can lead you down a dark road of depression, withdrawal, and anxiety.

But you shouldn't entirely blame your family for this emotional shutdown. I want you to think of your family as a busy city with tons of streetlights and rules for the pedestrians and cars. When racism happens to a family and that family doesn't have the tools to heal—the ability to name what's happened, to deal with the feelings that result, and to keep what happened from happening again—the trauma is like a power outage that causes the lights to flicker, maybe even to turn entirely off in some places, and makes it harder for the city to run the way it should.

In other words, without proper coping skills the experience of racial trauma can be long and painful; in fact, it can last for many generations. As you will learn in chapter 2, intergenerational trauma is what happens to families who stay in a state of depression, withdrawal, and anxiety without self-awareness and coping skills. Intergenerational trauma can affect how you see yourself, your family, and other people in the world. It also means that racism doesn't have to happen directly to you for you to feel its negative impact: intergenerational trauma can be passed down from your ancestors through what they share with you. For example, intergenerational trauma can be passed down from your great-grandmother to you if she constantly shares with you her own tragic experiences with racism. Racism can also affect families across generations through what it teaches parents and caregivers to do with their children. For instance, the racism your great-grandmother experienced may have affected the way she parented your grandfather, which affected the way he parented your father, which affects you in the present.

Have you had experiences like this growing up in your family? Over the course of my teen years, I learned that intergenerational trauma had impacted my family's ancestry and would impact the younger generations within my family as well. I began to see its effects in my family's attitudes and thoughts, behaviors and beliefs, choices and patterns, and political and cultural values. Just listening to some of the stories told by my great-grandparents and older aunts, uncles, and cousins revealed the intergenerational trauma I previously thought to be simply the way my family functioned. But once I could see the trauma in our past, and the ways it affected us, I began to understand what I could do about it.

As an adult I still experience racism in my personal and professional life. The only difference between who I am now and who I was as a teenager is that I have learned healthy coping and self-reflection skills.

Part 2 of this book will teach you these skills—practices like *cognitive restructuring* (noticing your negative thoughts and working to change them), *thought stopping* (learning how to catch negative thoughts before they go too far), relaxation and self-care, and more.

Keep in mind that you're not the only one who's experienced racism; you're not alone in how you feel. Throughout this book you will read short stories about Jasmine—a Black and mixed-race fourteen-year-old girl who comes from a family with intergenerational trauma. I met Jasmine—as a therapist—when she was ten years old and in a predominately White school.

Her parents are both multiethnic—her mother is Black and Latina and her father is Black with German heritage. Now it's your turn to meet Jasmine.

Jasmine felt isolated, anxious, and depressed when faced with racism. There were times Jasmine felt misunderstood by her peers—even those she thought were her best friends. Once when she stopped at the girls' bathroom to check her makeup after class, she overheard two of her best friends talking about a Black boy from the eleventh grade who spoke to them in the hallway on their way to lunch period. She heard one of the girls say, "I don't know why Ty'rell thinks he's the best on the football team. All Black boys are good at football. And rapping too!" She heard her other friend say, "Yes, and that's about it." Jasmine confronted them and asked why they would speak this way. She expressed to them that these words were hurtful.

Following this confrontation, Jasmine began to experience bullying. The first incident involved her ex-best friend intentionally ignoring her at lunch. The second incident involved someone posting an indirect racial meme on Instagram. The third incident involved Jasmine being pushed to the ground and having her backpack stolen.

As you will see in the following chapters, Jasmine struggled with racial trauma from such experiences—but she also learned the importance of learning and growing from these painful experiences, and to develop her self-worth apart from her experiences of racism. And she learned how important it was to get in touch with herself, her own racial identity—her sense of herself as a person in a particular racial group—and her own hopes and dreams, in a positive way.

And in the pages to come, you too will go on your own journey to heal from the impacts of racial trauma and protect yourself and your family from it in the future.

Starting Your Healing

Let's begin your journey to healing from racial trauma and building your sense of who you are and what you want and what is rightfully yours to own. In the chapters to come, you'll learn valuable skills that you can make part of your day-to-day life, and you'll reflect on important questions.

I encourage you to keep a notebook handy so you can work through these exercises—and write down the emotions that might arise as you read to think about why you are feeling them. Doing this will help you reflect upon your experiences and commit what you learn to memory.

You will be able to learn and practice all the activities in this book in your everyday life to help you heal. For example, you can practice being aware of your negative thoughts about yourself and your race by acknowledging the thoughts and then writing them down in your notebook. You can also practice relaxation and self-care to help you relieve stress.

Let's get started on chapter 1, in which we'll explore more about what racial trauma is and how it affects us. That's where the work of healing will begin. Remember, it is okay to have a lot of emotions as you read through this book. Racial trauma is a very difficult topic—especially when you can relate to the subject you are reading about.

PART 1

What We Mean When We Talk About Racial Trauma

CHAPTER 1

Your Individual Experience

Do you ever feel like the trauma you have experienced—the experience of racism or struggle in your family—has made you a different person from your peers? Do you feel like you see life in a different way because of that trauma?

Racism can affect everything in your life. It can affect how you see yourself, how you see other people, how you appreciate your culture, how you approach the world, and how you describe yourself to others. You can heal from trauma if you work hard to find healthy coping skills that can reverse the effects it causes—shame, anger, grief, stress, a sense you don't matter. But first you must acknowledge it and accept it: come to understand it, so that you can see how it has affected your life. Doing this helps you fully understand your trauma and ultimately grow from the pain of racism.

In this chapter, we will explore what racial trauma is and how we come to experience it as individuals. We'll also talk about the impact of racial trauma—how it affects your body, and how it affects your mind. Finally, we will discuss post-traumatic stress disorder (PTSD), which is one conse-quence of racial trauma when it's severe or when you experience it for a long time, and the negative consequences of racial trauma on your overall development.

Your Traumatic Experience

Being a Black or mixed-race person can be difficult. You may feel pressured to always meet other people's expectations—especially the expectations of people who don't look like you. Perhaps the expectations of teachers, coaches, dance instructors, and other adults in your world seem to be too much. Your peers may hold high expectations of you that make you feel inadequate. What's more, you may struggle with low self-esteem and uncertainty about your abilities and your intelligence because of the images you see around you about your race. You may be the only Black or mixed-race person in your grade—or possibly your entire school. You may feel alone or isolated in your after-school activities if you are the only Black or mixed-race kid there. All these experiences are racial experiences that can be stressful to go through, and that may stay with you for a very long time. And the stress they cause can lead you to have negative thoughts about yourself and the world around you—and to feel like you're less than the people around you. For example, during class discussions you may begin to feel left out by your classmates and the teacher as well. This feeling could cause you to think negatively about your abilities as a student. You may begin to think, *I'll never get a good grade in this class; My teacher never calls on me to participate in class discussions like she does the other kids;* or *My teacher doesn't like me.* These negative thoughts can be reinforced by your teacher's attitude during the week or the B she gave you on your most recent assignment.

Racial trauma is defined as the experience of repeatedly encountering prejudice, racism, or discrimination that negatively impacts your ability to function in your daily life. One of the big problems with racial trauma, and the negative impact of racism, is that we don't often talk about it. Most of us were never taught how. In the end, your racial experiences should be put into words to help you identify how you really feel.

Sadly, the reason we don't talk much about racism is because we don't always understand it or why it is happening. When you experience racism and have a hard time understanding why you are being treated a certain way, it's often easier to just ignore your feelings and keep going. But if you withdraw into your own world and avoid open communication about what you are feeling, you are doing something known as *internalizing*. To internalize your experience is to keep your feelings and experiences inside rather than expressing them, which makes them difficult to process and deal with. Internalizing your experience of racism can lead to anxiety and depression. And these feelings go on to affect the ways you behave—sometimes in ways you don't even realize. For instance, anxiety and depression can cause you to second-guess yourself and place blame on yourself. You may begin to ask yourself if the racial trauma has occurred because of something you did or did not do. You may question why a particular racist incident happened and if it will happen again.

When racism occurs, it can be difficult to develop a clear understanding of why it is happening. Opening up about your experience is the first step toward really understanding it and being able to move past it. Asking yourself questions like these can help you take that step: Have you experienced a situation where you felt you were being treated unfairly because of racism? What did you think and feel at that time?

If you experience racial trauma repeatedly and over extended periods of time, it can turn into something known as *complex trauma*, a particular form of trauma that can happen when you experience a long-term trauma, or multiple traumas, that you can't escape. It's related to racial trauma, but also different: racial trauma can come from a single incident you experience, while complex trauma often comes from a long-term experience of racism, or the long-term experience of growing up in a family affected by racism. You can also experience this form of trauma—perhaps in your relationships or in your family as a Black or mixed-race person, and feel trapped, imprisoned, terrified, or defeated by the situation for many years.

Think of complex trauma as a severe form of PTSD for individuals and a severe form of intergenerational trauma for families. You, or your family, may experience complex trauma differently from other people. You may notice memory loss of the traumatic experience, feeling detached from your body, internalized anger, or time-limited traumatic stress—meaning a very brief but intense feeling of shock and fear.

Because racism is difficult to escape and may happen in many areas of your life, it is possible for you to experience complex trauma for the rest of your life. For example, let's say you grew up in a neighborhood where you always felt unsafe as the only Black or mixed-race person. If you experienced being bullied and feeling unsafe not just once, growing up, but a lot, you could experience fear, anxiety, headaches, feeling shaky, and other signs of stress—which are all common symptoms of complex trauma. Sometimes you may even have these symptoms when there's nothing stressful going on in the world around you.

One particularly common form of racism we experience in our everyday lives—which can trigger or intensify our stress—is racial messages or microaggressions. Let's take a closer look at racial messages and microaggressions.

Racial Messages and Microaggressions

Racial messages are the messages people and society at large often give us about how worthy people of different racial groups are. Sometimes these messages are overt; they're given to you through words or actions that are clearly racist, like being stereotyped, profiled, or harassed because of the color of your skin. Sometimes they're more subtle. You might hear racial messages about these areas (Sue et al. 2007):

- Cultural values—whose customs or patterns of behavior are seen as better or more normal. (Often, in American culture, customs or patterns of behavior that are assumed to be linked to White culture are seen as "normal." Customs and patterns of behavior that are seen as Black, or particular to any other race, are seen as abnormal or denigrated. Sometimes they're exoticized, which means they're seen as cool or glamorous, but in a way that's stereotyped, not genuine.)

- Intelligence—which races are assumed to be smarter than others.

- Criminality—which races are assumed to be "dangerous," and which are not.

- Status—what kind of treatment people of different races are entitled to in stores, restaurants, banks, and other public places.

One example of a subtle racial message is a microaggression. As you read earlier, microaggressions are described as statements or actions that are indirect or hidden but contain within them discrimination, racism, or prejudice against members of a marginalized race or group.

Racial messages and microaggressions include statements such as these:

- "You speak really well to be Black."

- "Most Black people are really hard to understand but you're easy to understand."

- "Are you Black? Are you biracial? What's your race? You don't look like a Black person."

- "Your hair is great. Can I touch it?"

- "Your hair is so cool. How do you get it that way? Why is it so puffy?"(while pointing at your natural hair shrinkage)

- "How do you pronounce your name again: Kyriee, Qieree, or Kylie?" (correct name: Kyriee).

- "I don't think you would like going with me to this concert because of the type of band playing. But I'm going to a rap concert on Friday. Wanna go?"

- "Why isn't your dad ever home?"

- "My mom said your mom is a single mom who's struggling to make ends meet."

- "I didn't know you dated other races. I thought you were just into the Black boys."

You'll see that a lot of these statements depend on particular ideas of who Black people are and what they "usually" do or like. The speakers also don't respect boundaries. Some of the statements are even shaming in nature, though they may not be meant that way.

Ultimately, racial messages and microaggressions can come in many forms. And microaggressions, in particular, can be so subliminal, so hidden that you may not be able to detect them until long after you've heard them. Some people who display microaggressions aren't even aware they're doing it. But if you can learn to understand what they sound like and how they can affect you, you can begin to fight back against the impact they can have on your life.

Reflection: Can you think of any microaggressions you've experienced in the past? Or any racial messages people have transmitted to you through their words or their actions?

Recognizing microaggressions and racial messages takes practice and requires reflection. So, if you find it hard to think of any, that's fine. Just keep giving it thought so you can understand and begin to process the things that might happen to you before they cause lasting trauma.

It may also help to read through Jasmine's experience with racial messages. As you read, see if you can find the racial messages Jasmine's been exposed to.

I'm the only Black and mixed-race person in my grade. I go to a school where there aren't a lot of people who look like me. I feel alone most days and I don't know if I'm accepted by most people in my school. I even question whether the teachers like me.

One day I was late, and in front of the whole class Mr. Kelvin asked me why I was late every day. I was very embarrassed, but I told him that my mom just had my baby sister, and she cries a lot at night. He told me that my mom should make sure I get better sleep at night so that I'm on time and my grades improve.

Then I was putting my books away in my locker to go to lunch period when a kid walking by me whispered the N-word under his breath. He's a White kid from the football team. He thinks it's funny to call names because it makes him look powerful to his teammates. I told him to stop but he just kept doing it. In the lunchroom, he had the entire table laughing. I couldn't take it anymore, so I left and ate my lunch in the library.

While I ate, I asked the librarian if she could tell me where to find a book about the Freedom Riders and their trip from Virginia to New Orleans. She asked if I was doing a research project and I told her that I wasn't, but I wanted to learn more about their experience with racism. She asked, "Why would you want to read such a sad book in the middle of the school day?" I told her that I felt it related to me in some way. She said, "You won't be able to relate to the Freedom Riders because you're not experiencing racism. The 1960s was a very sad time but all of that is over. Your life is much better than the Freedom Riders, because that kind of racism doesn't exist anymore."

I was very sad to hear her speak like this. Here I was dealing with racism in my school all alone, and she's telling me racism is over! It's not over. It still exists. It may not be the kind of racism the Freedom Riders experienced but it still hurts.

Reflection: Were you able to spot the racial messages Jasmine received? How have these messages affected her?

Do you hear similar ones from people around you? How have those affected you?

I encourage you to write down your own thoughts and feelings as you read about Jasmine's experience.

Another way to process how racial messages affect you is by asking yourself what are called existential or philosophical questions. In the next section, we will explore what this might look like.

The brain and body respond to stress in many ways, so it's very important to understand the signs that your particular body is giving you that you are under stress. Let's look at that now.

Reflection: Think back to a time when you experienced racism. What was your body feeling? What were you thinking?

The stress response often starts as a feeling or a thought that can trigger your body to react to protect you from the threat. In this case, the threat is racism. Once the brain senses that a threat is near, you may notice different changes in your body. These changes may include:

- Increased heart rate
- Racing thoughts or confusion
- Sweating or feeling hot
- Wanting to cry or breaking down in tears
- Heaving or shallow breathing
- Feeling dizzy or faint
- Sweaty hands or feet
- Butterflies in your stomach or nausea
- Tense muscles all over the body or in one or more areas
- Dry mouth and loss of appetite
- Quick and impulsive decision making
- Trouble holding urine or feces

Reflection: Can you identify the changes you feel in your body?

Once you understand the signs of stress, it is important to understand what triggers your stress. That knowledge is the first step toward learning how to engage your brake-pedal system in a conscious way—which can help you recover from racial trauma you might face and learn to cope with it.

Growing up as someone from a multiethnic background, I experienced years of challenges with discrimination and racism because of the differences in my family, my education (for example, being homeschooled), my hair, the tone of my voice, my skin, and the things I was able to achieve. Despite all this, I eventually learned how to cope with being seen as "different."

I also learned how to accept that the way certain people saw and responded to my differences could trigger a stress response in me when I least expected it. It could make me feel emotionally overwhelmed, self-conscious, and uncertain about how I approached other people or certain things in my life. My stress response caused me to see myself through the eyes of racism and discrimination. And having this knowledge actually helped me understand that what I was feeling wasn't my fault—and that I could do something about it, besides just struggling with it.

Once you learn to spot racial messages when they're transmitted to you, and understand how they're triggering your gas and brake pedals, how you will respond is up to you. And you have more power to respond than you know. Believing in yourself and in your ability to calm your body and your mind is sometimes all it takes to feel better. Responding to the fight-or-flight system gets easier as you learn what tools relax the brain and the body. It may not always feel like you can choose how to respond, but you can—especially when you come to understand how the experiences you have can influence your thoughts, feelings, and behaviors.

It's also worth knowing what can happen when you encounter racism and aren't able to address it. In the next few chapters, you will be able to learn about the connection between thoughts, feelings, and behaviors so that you can consciously choose a healthy response to direct and indirect racism in your life.

Post-Traumatic Stress Disorder

You can think of PTSD as being a more severe form of anxiety. If you are experiencing some of its symptoms, it is important to reach out for help. Let's start with Jasmine's experience. You'll see that she struggled with symptoms for a long time before reaching out for help.

I experience a lot of bullying from peers at school for "looking Black and speaking Spanish." And there are these three girls who've been causing trouble for me at school since the third grade. One day on my way home they stopped me on the street. They pushed me against a wall, teased me, called me racial slurs, and threatened me. They would also tease me in school and mock me as I walked toward my locker by the end of the school day.

These attacks were so scary. I had never been attacked for being who I am. It has been three months since it happened, and I've been having panic attacks, night terrors, and bad dreams. I haven't been able to walk anywhere alone, sleep, or enjoy hanging out with my friends. I told my mom I'm feeling afraid even when there's no apparent reason, and I can't relax. I feel like my heart's always beating faster, and my muscles feel so tight. I have a lot of headaches, and my stomach often feels sick. At school, I ask to be excused from class almost every day to sit in the nurse's office.

I sometimes get angry with people in a way I never used to, and I feel like I can't control it. I can't figure out why I'm so afraid to be me or how to make it stop. I don't sleep, I feel like I need to look over my shoulder all the time, and I cry in the bathroom almost every day in school.

When Jasmine told her school counselor about being bullied and then attacked by the three girls, the counselor explained that her experience was a stressor, and that because Jasmine had been feeling this way for over a month and couldn't seem to move past it, she might have PTSD. As they talked, they realized she had many symptoms of PTSD:

Intrusive symptoms: Jasmine could not get the experience of being jumped out of her mind and nothing could distract her from it for long.

Avoidance of experiences or activities you feel will be triggering: Jasmine avoided walking home from school alone and would only leave school if she knew one of her parents would be picking her up.

Changes in mood and thinking: Because she was beginning to feel helpless, Jasmine would experience a lot of fear and anger that she felt like she couldn't share with anyone. She also felt anxious and uneasy most of the time. She was preoccupied with fear, anxiety, and angry thoughts. She always felt the need to look over her shoulder.

Changes in how you respond to triggers and how intensely you respond: Jasmine would respond to everyone by yelling "What?!" She was not the calm and kind teen she used to be. She felt like she *couldn't* be. None of the changes in her mood or behavior were her fault. She couldn't control how she was reacting to things. She struggled with coping with trauma triggers all around her, which caused her to lash out at times. She felt like a different person.

Duration: Jasmine's symptoms lasted for over a month and caused her great distress. And over time, it became clear there were no other possible causes for her behavior. Her behavior could not be blamed on a bad night's sleep or teen irritability. Being "jumped" was the start of all these symptoms. And simple habit changes, like making sure she got plenty of sleep, weren't enough to make them go away.

As Jasmine and the counselor continued to talk, it became clear Jasmine was also experiencing dissociation when she was reminded of her trauma. *Dissociation* can take hold of you when you have PTSD. It's a feeling of zoning out, like you are daydreaming and can't stop. You may feel like you are detached from everything. You may experience *depersonalization*—feeling like you are watching yourself act in your own story or like you are detached from your body—or *derealization*—feeling like reality is not reality, almost like you are living in a fairy tale.

PTSD and Your Nervous System

Post-traumatic stress disorder is a mental health condition that impacts your central nervous system (CNS) and your autonomic nervous system (ANS). Although both systems are important in managing what I like to call your gas and brake pedal systems, the ANS—the system that controls your automatic bodily processes like breathing—is often triggered by anything that upsets, scares, or threatens you. Again, racism can trigger the fight-or-flight system, which is a part of the ANS. When triggered, the ANS results in increased heart rate, nervousness, hypervigilance, worry, feeling shaky, sweating, dizziness, and racing thoughts. PTSD includes all these symptoms.

When you experience repeated racial messages and microaggressions in your life without knowing how to process them properly, it can lead to trauma responses. Let's take a look at this now, starting with what the body goes through when faced with stressful experiences like the experience of racism—the stress response.

Your Stress Response—Fight, Flight, or Freeze

Your stress response is controlled by two systems in your body, the central nervous system and the autonomic nervous system. The central nervous system controls your movements, thoughts, and emotions. It includes the brain and the spinal cord, which is encased in the vertebrae (the bony segments that make up the spinal column). The second system, the autonomic nervous system, is the one that controls your body's automatic processes—for example, it helps you breathe,\ and swallow without effort—and it causes you to respond to stress. It can also be broken down into two other systems that influence your stress response: the sympathetic nervous system and the parasympathetic nervous system. The fight-or-flight response is triggered by what the brain believes is a threat—something that poses a danger to you in some way—and it allows you to either stay and face the threat or escape from it. When the brain perceives a threat, it triggers two important internal systems: your gas pedal and brake pedal.

Gas Pedal

The sympathetic nervous system is the gas pedal of the body; it speeds us up to help us fight anything we feel we need to fight. Our body is ready to attack whatever is encroaching upon us that feels unsafe. Sometimes we may even freeze out of fear and not know what to do to help ourselves get out of a threatening situation.

Often, when you face racism, your gas-pedal system can kick in. Symptoms of this happening include feeling on edge, increased heart rate, sweating, nervousness or shakiness, feeling overwhelmed, and feeling nauseated. You might find yourself getting agitated at the person or situation you're facing; you may begin to see the environment as well as other people as the enemy.

When you have a lot of experiences that trigger your body to hit the gas pedal, or when your gas-pedal system has been going too long, that's stressful in and of itself. If you experience the gas-pedal system repeatedly throughout your development because of racism, you may begin to show signs of PTSD. We'll talk more about that later in this book.

Brake Pedal

The parasympathetic nervous system is the body's brake pedal. It calms everything in your body after a threat has passed and helps your body return to its normal state. When your brake pedal is on, you may notice your heart rate decrease, your appetite return, your breathing pace slow down. You may also feel tired.

When your gas-pedal system is engaged, your body may struggle to reach the brake-pedal stage—especially if you are facing the same threat every single day. Racism—both the kind you may experience directly (such as someone using the N-word or some other racial slur) and the kind you may observe in your family (like your caregiver having a hard time at their job because of discrimination at their workplace)—is a daily threat that can keep your body in gas-pedal mode and make it difficult for you to calm down when the threat is gone. For example, if you experience microaggressions from peers in school, it can cause your body to sense the threat that this might happen again the next time you see those other students. You might go into fight-or-flight mode, and struggle to reach the brake-pedal stage even after those students have walked on by.

Reflection: Can you relate to Jasmine's experience of PTSD? Can you think back to a time when you were faced with a stressful situation and began to feel anxious, afraid, overwhelmed, or angry? Maybe you have these feelings often, and you feel like they make it hard for you to be happy or feel safe.

Moving Forward

I hope that from this chapter you have been able to see your own experiences more clearly, so that you will be better able to use the coping skills and strategies provided to you in the next chapters. We'll explore different skills that will help you with these experiences—like understanding your thoughts and the ways you typically talk to yourself so you can see if they're accurate, and learning how to break the patterns of thought and anxiety that can keep you stuck in a loop of shame and low self-worth because of the trauma you or your family have experienced. You will also learn about the process of grief and how to work through unresolved trauma.

Now that we have explored the impact racial trauma can have on your individual experience, let's look at the negative impact on your family experience.

CHAPTER 2

Your Family Experience

It may be hard to understand just how racism experienced by family members throughout generations can cause racial trauma. Experiences with racial trauma within your family that is hidden or secret can cause what is known as intergenerational family trauma. In this chapter, you will learn about racial trauma as it manifests in the family.

Trauma and PTSD in Your Family

Just like the PTSD Jasmine talked about in chapter 1, your entire family may experience the same symptoms at different times in their lives. For example, if your parent (I use "parent" to also refer to a guardian or caregiver, or anyone who takes care of you like a parent) worked in a predominantly White business where they were treated badly by the boss because of race and discrimination, they are likely to experience a stress response when they're around their boss or coworkers. If that racism and discrimination repeatedly happens for many years, they may begin to experience increased anxiety, hypervigilance (that is, feeling jumpy or feeling as though you need to constantly look over your shoulder), depression or sadness, increased heart rate, and anger—often the first signs of PTSD. This may go on to influence how they treat themselves, you, or other members of the family.

Racism in our environments is often made worse by how hard it can be to change our environments—to get a new job, for example. If you're not able to escape the racism and discrimination you face, it can lead to long-term damages—what we call complex PTSD (you'll find a full discussion of complex PTSD in chapter 8). And the symptoms of racial trauma we've experienced can influence the ways we parent and take care of the people we're responsible for.

I'm sure that when you hear stories of discrimination or racism from family members you have certain emotions that are hard to move past. Even just knowing that members of your family have felt confused, conflicted, or detached from the community because of the color of their skin can negatively impact you for years to come. This is known as *vicarious trauma*: the trauma you experience after observing or hearing about a traumatic experience someone else has experienced.

It's also worth knowing about other forms of trauma that can negatively affect you or family members and be passed on to many generations after you, because of the way trauma affects how we behave. Some examples of traumatic experiences that can be passed on include:

- The sudden or unexpected death of a loved one

- Experiencing domestic abuse

- Witnessing violence in the community

- A member of the family receiving a serious medical or mental health diagnosis

- Experiencing homelessness

- Difficulty finding the resources you need to recover because of racism, financial hardship, and other forms of adversity

- Being sexually assaulted or raped

- Car accidents or other travel-related accidents

- Having an incarcerated family member

- Separation from a parent or caregiver

- Severe physical injuries

- Experiencing natural disasters such as hurricanes, strong storms, or tornados, especially when unexpected

If you or your family have unresolved trauma from any of these experiences and there has not been a healing process—by which the person who experienced the trauma has been allowed to put it into words, share it with others, and get help to cope with what they feel, and isn't forced to resort to unhealthy methods of coping with the stress they're going through—it is likely that this trauma will be passed down to younger generations. When this happens, it is like a family heirloom that no one in the family really wants. Put another way, if you and your family have dealt with racism and racial trauma in the past, and your emotions around the trauma are unresolved, this can lead to intergenerational trauma.

More About Intergenerational Trauma

Intergenerational trauma is defined differently based on who you talk to. But essentially, it's trauma that has happened across different generations of a family, or that has been passed down within one's family to younger generations. Some people argue this trauma takes the form of specific conditions that get passed down through generations, such as physical conditions (for example, heart disease, asthma), behavioral or mental health problems, and substance abuse problems. But in general, it's agreed that this kind of trauma happens because of a traumatic event that began years prior to the current generation and has impacted the ways in which individuals within the family understand, cope with, and heal from that traumatic event and its aftereffects.

Intergenerational trauma can influence how your parents raise you and set the rules and boundaries in your household. For example, if every child in your extended family who has attended a public school experienced racism there, your parents may push for you go to a Black-owned private school—even if they have to overwork themselves to afford the tuition. Attending a Black-owned private school to help cope with racism and racial trauma may be perceived as *Afrocentrism*. Afrocentrism is something that happens when Black people adhere to the values and norms of only those who support the traditional African system of values, beliefs, and politics, and it can be a very unhealthy way to cope with racism and racial trauma. This kind of mindset is the result of negative patterns of coping that continue for many generations—that is, intergenerational trauma. Past experience of racism leads to a fear of possibly experiencing racism again, and your parents become determined to act in ways that they think will help them avoid that outcome.

Another form of intergenerational family trauma is the continuation of abusive behavior throughout generations. Abusive behavior may include verbal/emotional abuse (for example, name calling, yelling or screaming, threatening, belittling), physical abuse (for example, hitting, kicking, biting, pinching, slapping), and sexual abuse.

Abusive behavior may show up in your relationship with your parent(s) or you may observe it happening between your parents. You may also notice abusive behavior between siblings, cousins, and other extended family members. Because trauma impacts how you respond to stress and how you see the world, abusive behavior can develop over the years within a family.

Note: It's important to know that if you're dealing with abuse of any kind in your family, you should do your best to seek help. Talk to an adult you trust who can give you advice about what to do. It may be hard to reach out to someone about things like this, but you deserve to be safe, healthy, and happy, as do the people you love. And no one deserves to be abused or mistreated. I know this can be difficult to do—and not every situation is easy to seek help for. But it is important for you to know that you matter and so does your safety.

Again, it may be helpful to think of your family as operating like a busy city, with rules, beliefs, and patterns that influence their view of life and can impact how they handle intergenerational trauma. Sometimes traumatized families create "hidden" rules that dictate how trauma will be managed within the family. For example, your great-grandmother may be so disturbed by the trauma she experienced growing up that she sends a silent message through body language and attitude (such as looking down and avoiding eye contact or turning her body away from the person she is talking to) that she doesn't want to talk about it. Everyone in the family may avoid the topic to help her keep it a secret. This avoidance is meant to be good for your great-grandmother and for the family—it can even be meant as a gesture of love. But in the long run, the secrecy only perpetuates the trauma. A family cannot function like a healthy system if negative patterns of behaviors, thoughts, and feelings are never addressed.

Let's look at the signs that can help you tell if your family is struggling with intergenerational trauma.

Signs of Intergenerational Trauma

You may be wondering what signs you could look for that would tell you your family has experienced intergenerational trauma. The main thing to look for is *negative coping*—certain patterns of behavior that are unhealthy and problematic, and reflect stress and trauma that a person hasn't really processed.

Unresolved Emotions and Thoughts

If you know that trauma—experiencing microaggressions; experiencing overt discrimination and prejudice from others; suffering from discrimination in housing, in access to healthcare, in relations with the legal system; experiencing police violence directed at people of color—has occurred in your family, and no one in your family ever really talks about it, it is easy to bury it and function as if nothing ever happened. Families that do this have unresolved emotions and thoughts that have never been addressed. Secrets and taboo topics are then created and perpetuated throughout many generations.

Negative Behavior

Negative patterns of behaving can continue for generations if they are not correctly identified and addressed. For example, if your father believes that because of structural racism there is no benefit to trying hard to make something of himself, he may pass this mindset, and its resulting behavior, on to you.

Untreated or Poorly Treated Mental Health Needs

People in families that haven't really addressed traumatic experiences may end up using substances like drugs or alcohol in ways that aren't so healthy to numb what they're feeling, or make it easier to get through the day. It can also be hard to address mental health issues; sometimes, these issues are normalized, ignored, or not taken as seriously as they should be. If drugs or alcohol is normalized in your family and you notice several generations in your family abusing these substances, intergenerational trauma may be to blame. Some families with intergenerational trauma may also struggle with generations of family members who have had suicidal thoughts—thoughts of wanting to die. There are two kinds of thoughts that may happen if help is never sought: passive suicidal thoughts (thoughts like "I wonder what never waking up would be like") and direct suicidal thoughts (thoughts like "I am going to overdose on pills"). Sometimes suicidal thoughts are experienced by someone who wants to escape the pain they feel. If their pain is never dealt with, that person may begin to experience suicidal thoughts.

Note: If you are experiencing suicidal thoughts, it's important to seek help. It can be hard to share your thoughts and feelings with others but the only way you are going to get help is by asking for it. A first step toward asking for help begins with the National Suicide Prevention Lifeline—1-800-273-8255—or you can begin a chat at www.suicidepreven tionlifeline.org.

Poor Relationship with Your Parent(s)

Our relationships with our parents form the basis for what scientists call *emotional attachment*—which is a fancy term for being able to form healthy emotional connections with other people, and to build meaningful relationships for ourselves. Basically, from the time we're babies, we learn by the way our parents treat us as we're growing up that we are safe and loved. But if your family has intergenerational trauma, and your parent has unresolved issues that have never been addressed, they may not be able to form a healthy attachment with you. They may not be able to show you that they see and understand what you feel, really take care of you when you're upset, and more. Sometimes, they may not have had these opportunities from their own parents. As a result, their relationships—and potentially yours—can suffer.

Complicated Personalities

When trauma is hidden within a family, it can be difficult to figure out why certain of your family members behave as they do; you may even find yourself shocked by some of their behaviors. Unresolved trauma may cause a lot of behavioral and personality problems in your family. For example, major depression, anxiety disorders, phobias and fears, and ADHD can cause academic, employment, and social problems that make it hard to function in society. You may notice changing moods, irritability, fear of change, and a generally negative view of things in family members like this.

Wanting to Give Up

If intergenerational trauma has impacted your family, you may notice that some family members want to give up and accept things the way they are—which may not be very good. You may notice that some family members give up more easily than you might want them to. It's understandable to feel confused by this behavior, or even resentful of it. But it's important to remember that this can be a way for a person to make whatever peace they can with things they have little control over. And sometimes what seems like giving up is not necessarily giving up. Sometimes it's an act of acceptance and choosing to move on in their life. Or sometimes it's a person doing the best they can do given the circumstances. Like all painful experiences, it's something you should try to deal with as empathically as possible—even as you seek to avoid those patterns in yourself.

Reflection: As you can see, there are many ways intergenerational trauma can be displayed in your family. Do any of these seem like things your family is dealing with?

Fear of Rejection

When I was thirteen, I did a DNA ancestry test and some research on my family ancestry, and I learned that we had not only a biracial heritage but also a multiethnic heritage that sometimes caused tension within my family. My aunt has a mixed-race father and when she was growing up she was teased for having a "White daddy." She felt rejected and ashamed, and these feelings caused my family to ignore who we really are. Tension around our race and cultural history followed many generations in my family and began to negatively affect me growing up. When I applied to a university in a predominantly White upper-class area, I felt like some family members didn't think it was possible for me to get in because of my race. One person made a comment about me attending a "mixed university" and asked why I would ever consider that. As I reflect on that experience now, I know that this thinking was motivated by fear of rejection for being different and by years of experiencing racial trauma.

So the pattern of intergenerational trauma that I have noticed in my family is fear of rejection. If I were to journal this myself, I would write down where I think this discouragement and fear of rejection may have come from and how it impacts my life today.

> **Reflection:** Take a second to journal about any aspects of intergenerational trauma you notice in your family. These journal prompts may help you get started:
>
> What is a common theme or pattern in my family that may be considered intergenerational trauma?
>
> How far back in my family history does this intergenerational trauma go?
>
> Who in my family has experienced direct trauma, and how did it impact them?
>
> Did my family get help or support for intergenerational trauma?

Let's take a look at how intergenerational trauma has negatively impacted Jasmine's family.

It sounds a little silly to say it now—like, of course a Black person in America in the 1950s and '60s would have experienced racism. But I still couldn't quite believe it when my grandmother told me that she experienced racism growing up. I thought I was the only one in the family. And she's such a sweet person that it felt impossible to imagine anyone treating her badly. But she told me about a traumatic experience that caused her to avoid her peers and stay inside. She was the daughter of a mixed-race couple, and she struggled her entire life with fitting in. My grandmother grew up in a predominately White neighborhood where she was picked on for being light skinned and having really coarse hair. When the other kids found out that her father was White, they bullied her even more. I remember her telling me that these kids didn't appreciate her for her skills, intelligence, artistic ability, and interest in playing musical instruments for the school's theater production. It was like all they saw was her skin and her hair.

Despite the fact that my mother was considered light skinned by her peers, and therefore more accepted than my grandmother had been, she was still considered "too dark" by most people. She experienced being accepted by some people and rejected by others. Her skin tone determined what she could and could not do within her own race and outside her race as well. And she also felt like all her life she struggled to be appreciated and respected for her abilities. For instance, she wasn't encouraged to perform in theater or ballet because she didn't have a lot of Black role models to learn from. She wasn't encouraged to try out for the football team's cheerleading squad because she wasn't liked by many of the White peers on the team. My mother told me that things improved a bit in college, but that it was hard not to feel like this improvement came about because the school needed to prove they were not racist.

My grandmother and my mother suffered from low self-esteem, doubts, depression, loneliness, anxiety, and acceptance of who they were as Black and mixed-race women. Because of the fears they had about colorism (favoring people with lighter skin) discrimination, and prejudice, it seems like they want me to embrace the ideas, behaviors, styles, attitudes, and belief systems that represent only Black people. They told me they wanted me to have cultural pride—but I feel like my identity as a person isn't what I really want it to be.

In some ways, racism is like a virus, and once it attaches to someone it can be difficult for that person to recover from it. Thankfully, there are support systems for people and families dealing with racism. Humans exist, not alone, but as part of large community systems that can provide a lot of support when it's needed. It can help to think about family ecosystems—the systems, organizations, and people in your family's environment that can help you stay strong, deal with racial trauma and other forms of trauma, and weather the racism and difficult experiences you might face in the future.

Recognizing the Supports in Your Family's Ecosystem

If you are a Black or mixed-race person you can probably relate to Jasmine's family trauma. Yet despite the negative impact of racism on your family, you can probably look around and identify a lot of people and organizations that support your family in positive ways; for example, your church or religious affiliation, neighbors, friends and family, school and work, after-school activities and organizations, social clubs and sports teams, community mental health centers and clinics, coaches and mentors, or your family doctor or pediatrician. Knowing that these systems exist to support you and your family can make the process of recognizing racial trauma and healing from it a bit easier.

You may also find yourself feeling unsupported by these same systems—and that's okay. In that case, being able to identify why these systems aren't supporting you can build your awareness in powerful ways.

In the activity below, you will be able to reflect upon the systems that surround your family and to determine whether your family has experienced racism or support through these systems.

ACTIVITY 1: CREATE A FAMILY ECOMAP

A family ecomap is a great visual tool to help you think about the different environments and people in your life that support you or make your life harder, and how. For example, you and your family may go to church every Sunday for inspiration and peace of mind, which makes church a positive social system in your life. You may feel supported, loved, and cared for in this system known as the church. However, the church can also be a negative influence on your life if the people there are racist and judgmental.

At http://www.newharbinger.com/50126, you'll find the ecomap Jasmine created for herself as she considered whether the people and systems around her do or don't support her family, as well as a blank ecomap you can use to create your own. If you prefer, you can make your map in your journal.

These people and systems may be part of your ecosystem. Some will apply to you, some won't.

Your family

Your school

Your place of work

Your place of worship

Your friend group

Your extended family

Your therapist or doctor

Are there any others that aren't on this list? Add them to your ecomap.

These questions can help in creating your ecomap:

Are any of these people or systems ones with whom you or your family have experienced racism?

Are any of these people or systems ones who have supported you or your family?

How would being supported by each of these systems positively impact you or your family?

How would not being supported by each of these systems negatively impact you or your family?

As a Black or mixed-race person, how do these systems make you feel?

Jasmine's map showed her that she has some strong sources of support. Her family is a great source of encouragement and solace. Her coworkers are like another family in how they accept and support her, and she really likes the job too. Her doctor is someone she's known for a long time and trusts. And the pastor at her church feels like a person she can trust. There are also some environments where Jasmine really feels isolated and alone: at school, where she encounters bullies; with neighbors who sometimes make her feel uncomfortable; with her coach, who's sometimes unfair to her; and with well-meaning friends who just don't always understand what she goes through as a Black kid.

As she looked at all this together, Jasmine decided that she'd try to talk to her pastor more often. She also thought about sharing more about what she was feeling and thinking with her trusted coworkers, who she knew cared about her. She even considered sharing some things with her coach, who she had spoken to in the past before and after games. Their support might make it easier to deal with people at school who she felt disrespected her.

Each of these influences in your life serves an important purpose—to encourage and support you and your future in healing from racial trauma. You can also use the ecomap to help you identify the kinds of supports you need that you don't currently have. For example, if you have neighbors or a coach who supports you and who you feel close to, that is an important social connection that can help you overcome racial trauma. But if you don't have the support of your school or place of worship, for example, then you will want to consider if you would benefit from establishing a relationship with either or both. Without a strong connection to the supportive systems from the ecomap it is likely that you and your family could feel alone and isolated, which could make healing from racial trauma difficult.

You can use colors (such as red, green, and yellow) to help you identify the systems you have a relationship with and the systems you would like to strengthen or build a relationship with. For example, green would indicate a positive relationship, yellow would indicate a relationship that needs improvement, and red would indicate no relationship to the system at all.

Sometimes the use of social supports from the community is all that is needed for you to understand what you're going through, figure out healthy and proactive ways to deal with it—and remind yourself of your self-worth—and heal from racial trauma. A first step in healing from racial trauma might include self-care activities such as journaling, exercise, dance, art, and music. You can also use poetry, yoga, and martial arts to help you express yourself and develop self-confidence. At the very least, these will give you strength as you continue to understand the effects racial trauma has on your thoughts, feelings, and behaviors, and learn to undo them.

Moving Forward

You may not understand yet what it will take to heal from intergenerational trauma. Things may seem too difficult to change. But it isn't impossible with the right tools, perseverance, and courage.

In the next chapter, we will look at how your perception of yourself in the world can change how you feel, think, and behave. We will discuss racial identity or who you are because of your race, your self-talk or what you say to yourself, cognitive distortions or mental traps, and emotional injury—so we can begin rebuilding a sense of confidence, self-worth, and personal strength where racism may have compromised that in your life and in your family.

CHAPTER 3

How Racism Impacts Your Self-Image

Racism can take quite a toll on your mental health. It can make you feel like a totally different person. Your confidence may be shaky, your outlook on life may be dim, and your overall feeling of belonging and safety may have disappeared.

It's no wonder that so many people try to avoid the topic of racism. As you probably felt at some point in reading the last few chapters, it's uncomfortable. It's scary. But it's important to understand why you feel the way you feel so that you can fix it and learn to deal with whatever life might bring you. That's how you keep racism from making you feel like the problems you face are insurmountable or that you don't matter.

Understanding who you are begins with understanding your racial identity and your personal thoughts.

What Is Racial Identity?

Racial identity can be defined as your sense of self or who you classify yourself to be as a member of a racial group—for instance, Black or African American, White, Asian American, Native Hawaiian or Pacific Islander, and more. You can also identify as a member of multiple racial groups—that is, as multiracial. You most likely have a sense of attachment, of belonging or emotional connection, to the members of the racial groups you identify with; you feel a sort of kinship with them.

Racial identity also develops when other people classify you as being a part of a certain racial group. For example, although I am light in skin tone I would be classified by most people who see me as Black. Sometimes, these classifications can be simplifications. For instance, if you dig deeper into my racial identity, you will find that my heritage/race is also Native American, Northern African, and German. Ultimately, racial identity is multifaceted.

Did you know that the term "racial identity" has no biological basis? There isn't a single set of genes, for instance, that mark a person as Black or White or Asian or anything else. Put another way, you aren't born assigned to a specific race. Your race is assigned meaning by a group of people who all agree on what that racial term should mean. This means that in a racist society, everyone is assigned a race category that does not fully describe who they are (National Museum of African American History and Culture 2022). And what we call "racism" is the consequence of this phenomenon. That is, it's the result of having these arbitrary divisions between people that we call "races"—and using these categories to determine who is and isn't worthy.

The concept of racial identity has served the purpose of establishing rules, power, and privilege in our society. These rules have made it difficult for Black or mixed-race people to live freely. For example, you may feel like you must prove yourself to others repeatedly before you will be accepted. You may also feel like you will never experience the life that your White peers are experiencing—such as access to better things—just because of how the world perceives you. These feelings are normal and understandable because we live in a society where people of different races are stereotyped—described as having particular qualities—and we organize society based on race. And for many years in our society, race has been used as a means to control and oppress Black people most of all. This was done in blatant ways, like the four hundred years during which Black people were enslaved. It has also been used to marginalize Black people in subtle ways in the years since slavery ended—keeping them from opportunities, housing, employment, and many other things.

The flip side of this is that understanding what racial identity is, and claiming your racial identity as something you love about yourself and take pride in, is a meaningful act. It's a courageous step toward valuing who you are.

It's also worth keeping in mind that however you may be feeling about your racial identity—whether it's something you sometimes feel judged for, something you take pride in, or both of these things at different times—this identity is just one part of you. There's so much more to you to appreciate and be proud of—despite what you may have heard. One way to respond to racism is by understanding how it impacts your sense of self-worth.

Black and mixed-race people are often categorized based solely on the color of their skin. Being judged by the color of your skin can also mean you're wrongly judged in other areas of your life, such as where you live, how much money you have, what school you go to or what job you have, and more.

These judgments can lead to a lot of emotional and psychological pain in your life. For example, because of the color of your skin your friends may judge you unfairly and make comments that are hurtful without considering how these comments may make you feel. Or they may make statements about where you live, not considering that it may hurt your feelings to hear them refer to your home as "the ghetto." If you experience their comments repeatedly you may begin to feel shocked, disliked, and mistreated. This can lead to racial trauma. And it can cause you to feel like you're inferior in some way, like you have no worth, or like life will always be this way.

So what do you do when you feel like you are being wrongly categorized because of your racial identity—the color of your skin? Learning how to understand your own thoughts and work with them can positively impact how you respond to and cope with racism.

Cognitive Behavioral Therapy

The form of therapy known as *cognitive behavioral therapy*, or CBT, teaches us that the thoughts we have drive our behaviors, and the consequences of our behaviors go on to change our thoughts, in an ongoing cycle. When you begin to feel unfairly judged and disliked, your thoughts may become negative. Your thoughts, when they are negative, can trigger negative emotions—anger, sadness, hopelessness, and helplessness—and cause you to feel depressed or anxious in ways that ultimately affect how you react to things. For example, if the way you see Black people portrayed in the world makes you think to yourself that sometimes you don't even want to be Black, you may begin to feel insecure, embarrassed, or angry. These emotions can cause you to behave in ways that are not healthy, such as by isolating and withdrawing from others, or refusing to embrace your race—denying a fundamental part of yourself.

Of course, there's a flip side to this. If thoughts, feelings, and behaviors are all linked in this way, it also means that changing your mind and altering your behaviors can have a major impact on your sense of yourself and how worthy you are. While you will face hard things in life, and you can't always control how you feel, you don't *have* to react in anger or feel sad all the time. You can choose to react in a way that is healthy for you by recognizing what is happening, identifying your immediate emotions, and making a conscious choice to change your thoughts or your behavior to avoid unhealthy responses based on racial trauma.

One way to change your thoughts and your behavior is by changing your self-talk.

Self-Talk

Self-talk is basically the statements, either positive or negative in nature, that you say to yourself. These kinds of statements can negatively affect how you feel about yourself and about your race. But when you are able to identify the negative things you are saying to yourself—and identify them as not necessarily being true, because often they aren't—you can separate yourself from the negative self-talk.

ACTIVITY 2: CHANGE SELF-TALK FROM NEGATIVE TO POSITIVE

In this activity, we'll practice identifying your negative self-talk and changing it to reflect a more balanced perspective of things as they are. We'll start with some examples in different categories of experience.

Your appearance

Negative: "I hate my hair. It just won't stay straight. I feel like everywhere I go, people are judging me. I know the kids at school are wondering why my hair puffs up sometimes."

Positive: "My hair is a part of me that I can't ignore. I can learn about my hair texture and how to care for it better."

Your ability to achieve (as a Black or mixed-race teen, compared to your peers who are not Black or mixed-race)

Negative: "I know I'm going to be rejected if I try to get into Parish Academy. I'm Black, and there aren't a lot of kids like me in that school. No one will ever give me a chance. Black people are never given fair chances, so why should I try?"

Positive: "Some people won't like me as a person and that isn't my fault. All I can do is be the best person I can be and be kind to everyone I meet. Even when things get tough and I feel like no one likes me, I can find support with the people who do like me."

Fitting in

Negative: "I won't ever fit in at school because I'm the only kid who's not White. I'm not going to talk to anyone there. I'm just going to stay to myself."

Positive: "Sometimes it can feel lonely when I am the only person of color in school, but I might fit in just fine with some of the kids who like some of the things I like. I'll try to speak to at least one person who doesn't look like me every day."

Now, it's your turn. At http://www.newharbinger.com/50126, you can download a worksheet to use for your own self-talk. Take some time to make a list of negative things you say to yourself about your experiences being Black or mixed-race, and then change each to a positive statement.

Remember: you're not alone in experiencing these kinds of thoughts. Many of us who live in a society structured by racism have this sort of self-talk. It's also easy to believe the thoughts you have are the truth, especially when you have them often— when it's like you're being harassed by your own thoughts. But a lot of our negative self-talk is based on cognitive (or thought) distortions.

Cognitive Distortions

Cognitive distortions are "twisted" ways we think about things based on bad experiences we've had or false ideas that we have created unconsciously. These distortions twist your reality into something that may not be 100 percent true. For example, Jasmine was recently walking to the cafeteria and saw a girl she didn't know at all give her what seemed like a mean look. Her mind instantly leaped to the thought: *Why would she look at me like that? I must have done something wrong, or maybe she's friends with those girls who threatened me.* But while it's true that some of Jasmine's peers do bully her and cause a lot of emotional distress, that doesn't mean all her peers dislike her, or are united in harassing her in a racist way. When Jasmine leaps to the assumption that some of her peers being mean to her means that all of them dislike her, she's thinking in a way that may not actually be accurate.

In a society that may constantly be sending you the message that you are not strong, smart, capable, and worthy, it is important for you to learn how to identify the kinds of thoughts these messages can cause. When your mind begins to absorb messages from your environment—from school, friends, peers, and social media —it explores these messages to determine if they are useful or not. When the mind determines that a message is negative and difficult to process—such as overhearing peers in school using the N-word—it uses cognitive distortions as a defense mechanism or a way of protecting ourselves against stress.

Again, our minds are built to help us cope with the things we experience. And this is a very normal thing for the brain to do. But when we experience racism or family trauma, it sometimes leads our minds to think in ways that aren't actually helpful to us, or an accurate reflection of our lives as they actually are.

Do you sometimes feel that you are experiencing things like the following?

Generalization: Taking one negative situation or experience and believing that all experiences will be the same way

For example, Jasmine may believe that because she's been harassed by one group of students at her school, she'll be harassed by all the students at her school. Or she may believe that because she experienced bullying in her school, she will also experience it in her neighborhood.

Emotional reasoning: Believing that your emotions control your reality

Jasmine may begin to feel that because she is mixed-race, she doesn't offer anything positive to the world around her. She may believe this is 100 percent true just because her emotions are causing her to feel this way, even if there's clear evidence of the positive things she does offer her family, for example, or her friends at work.

Fortune telling: Predicting what will happen in a particular situation without truly knowing what will happen

Jasmine may predict that she will be bullied for the rest of her life, without thinking about whether this is accurate.

Negativity bias: Looking only at the negative in a situation rather than the positive

Jasmine may believe school is a very bad experience for her and completely forget that she has had some good days in school in the past.

All-or-nothing thinking: Seeing things in absolutes without considering that there may be other explanations

Jasmine may believe that because she is being bullied there must be something wrong with her without considering that perhaps something is wrong with her bullies instead.

Mind-reading: Believing that you know exactly what someone else is thinking about you

Jasmine may believe that a peer dislikes her just because she is staring at her and does not say hello in the hallway.

Minimization: Downplaying something that intimidates us when we don't feel confident or in control

Instead of being happy about getting an A+ on one of the hardest math tests of the school year, Jasmine may think, The only reason I got an A+ is because the teacher liked me. I was his favorite student.

Do you see any of your own thoughts in the examples above? Or do you see any of the distortions at work in the examples of negative self-talk you identified earlier? If these kind of thought patterns happen to you, that's okay. We all experience negative thoughts from time to time. Being Black or mixed-race in a society that has been influenced by racism can be very difficult. The key to overcoming these negative thoughts is by being able to recognize them and then change them to reflect reality.

To gain control over unhelpful negative thoughts, you can acknowledge within yourself that you are experiencing a certain emotion that is causing you to think negatively—and that this doesn't mean the thought and the feeling you are having reflects reality.

When you are struggling with negative thoughts, it's easy to find "evidence" to support them. Your goal is to counteract the "evidence" you believe you have. You don't want to lie to yourself, or simply push through painful feelings as though they're not based in an experience you're having—but you want to ask yourself if you are clearly seeing the situation you're in.

Learning to assess reality accurately is an especially important skill to practice when it comes to thoughts about how capable you are or whether you're good enough. Whether you're competing in an event or trying to learn a new skill, have you ever said to yourself, *I'm just not good enough* or *I can't fit in* or *I can't do anything right, I always mess up?* If so, did you notice your immediate emotion after making that statement? Did you feel discouraged or helpless?

Self-Fulfilling Prophecies

A *self-fulfilling prophecy* is something that you can make happen just by thinking or behaving as though it will happen. Often, when you say something negative about yourself out of anxiety or fear, or because of past experiences of racism or other difficulties, and you begin to feel negative, you actually behave in ways that end up setting you up for failure.

For example, let's say you are really good at speaking your mind and teaching other people things they don't know. One day you are faced with kids from your grade who say negative things about you because you are Black. You may find yourself saying things to yourself like *If they don't believe in me, why should I try to be good?* Or *These are some of the most popular kids in school. The fact that they don't like me is a big deal. No one will ever talk to me now.* Making these statements may cause you to isolate, withdraw, and appear insecure or closed-off to others, which can push other people away.

In this scenario, the students who mistreated you did indeed make it hard for you to feel confident about yourself. And what they did wasn't okay at all. But in the end, it wasn't those students who bullied you who made what they said about you true. You actually ended up behaving in ways that left you isolated, because it was hard for you to see that what those other students did to you was something *they* chose to do—it didn't necessarily reflect the situation as it was, or say anything about your self-worth.

Keep in mind that none of this is to excuse racism or other forms of mistreatment you might experience. And none of this is to say that you can simply think your way out of the things in your life that are hard, the things that make you feel discouraged and have painful thoughts. But it is a reminder that our thoughts can sometimes be distorted in ways that don't really help us deal with what we feel or meet hardship with strength. And if you can remember that your thoughts don't always reflect reality, you'll come to recognize when the thoughts you're having aren't all that helpful—when they might need to be challenged.

You want to stretch your thinking style so that you can make room for challenging those negative thoughts that may not be 100 percent correct. To challenge a negative thought would mean questioning yourself, your emotions, and your thoughts to determine if they are balanced or imbalanced. For example, when Jasmine saw her bullies in the lunchroom, her immediate thoughts were negative. One way Jasmine could have challenged her thoughts to determine if they were balanced would be to ask herself if her bullies may have been angry about something else that happened in school rather than being angry with her. She could have also asked herself why she cares if they don't like her. There are many ways to manage negative thoughts by challenging them.

As we have discussed so far, your thoughts, feelings, and behaviors are often influenced by how you are perceiving yourself in relation to others—or how you have learned to perceive situations in your life. As hard as it may seem to modify your thinking, it is worth the effort in the long run. Developing the ability to balance your thoughts is one way to heal from racial trauma.

Now let's look at something known as emotional injury so that you can fully understand how negative thoughts and cognitive distortions can affect you over time. You may not have symptoms of PTSD but you could be suffering from emotional injury—which is important to understand as you move through your healing journey.

Emotional Injury

Emotional injury can be defined as brief but overwhelming emotional distress, and it may happen to Black and mixed-race people who have experienced repeated racial trauma. The repeated experience of racial trauma reduces any confidence you may have had about yourself and may lead to cognitive distortions that cause depression and anxiety, but not PTSD. Although emotional injury can sound a lot like PTSD, it is a concept that describes a normal emotional response to a distressing event—such as witnessing something bad or unfair happening to someone you care about because of their race. Emotional injury occurs when you do not have the skills to help you cope in a healthy way. Without healthy coping skills, the mind begins to struggle with cognitive distortions to make sense out of the experience of racism.

An emotional injury is similar to a physical injury that causes pain and discomfort at first but may not feel so bad once it is bandaged. For example, you may have a paper cut that really hurts you and because you don't have anything to help you heal the wound it continues to cause you pain. It's only when you can bandage that wound that you begin to see it finally heal. Jasmine struggled a lot with the cognitive distortions that racial trauma causes. Let's look at her experience with emotional injury to help you better understand how it causes cognitive distortions.

I remember talking to my mother and grandmother about the way I was feeling after the bullying incident in school. I didn't like that I felt so ashamed of who I was just because of the color of my skin. I was feeling left out at school every day—especially when I overheard a girl in my class invite everyone to her sleepover but me. I tried not to think about it too much, but it was really hard. I thought maybe I did something wrong to her and couldn't remember. I questioned myself a lot. I thought maybe I was too different to be invited to her house. Or maybe her parents wouldn't like me. If she didn't like me and her parents didn't like me, who would ever like me? She's one of the most popular girls in school and she won't even look at me. I just feel so bad about myself that I want to hide. I don't want to go to school.

Reflection: Can you relate to Jasmine's story of emotional injury? Can you identify any cognitive distortions that she may have experienced?

If you're a Black or mixed-race person in a predominately White school or neighborhood, you probably know from experience how hard it can be. And even if you live in a diverse neighborhood or community, racism can make itself known in your life in other ways; you probably find yourself in contexts where it's hard not to feel all alone.

The best way to manage emotional injury is by finding healthy ways to cope with your experiences. One powerful coping skill is understanding your self-worth, which begins with understanding your history. It's important to know who you are. You may find yourself sometimes feeling unseen and without role models to feel proud of. But you don't have to feel that way. Keeping this truth in your heart can give you confidence and courage when you feel bad about who you are.

Your Family's Values

Our values guide us and keep us on track in our lives. They typically come from our parents, religious associations, cultural beliefs and influences, and school.

Racial trauma can have a negative impact on how you see yourself and your family, making it difficult to identify your family's values. Nevertheless, it's important to take a good look at those values so that you can examine what matters the most to you and which values make you who you are.

Your family's values say a lot about who you truly are and can help you build confidence and heal from racial trauma. The healing process also includes rebuilding your personal sense of values—spending some time exploring who you truly are.

ACTIVITY 3: FAMILY VALUES

In this activity, you will be able to write down the values that are most important to you and seem to be important to your family. You will also be able to identify words that may best describe your family.

I encourage you to write down your responses in your journal to help you keep track of your answers and reflect upon them later. You'll also find a worksheet at http://www.newharbinger.com/50126 for this activity.

- What are five important values that your family may hold?

- What is a value your parent told you was important to keep?

- If you had to choose the two most important values your family holds, what would they be?

- What are five of your own personal values?

- What values do you hold that your family had no influence over?

- Which adjectives in this list best describe your family, or specific members of your family, in a positive way?

Competent	Caring
Loving	Fair
Compassionate	Honest
Trustworthy	Creative
Dependable	Talented
Kind	Supportive of each other
Smart	Funny or humorous
Intelligent	Responsible
Takes initiative	Organized

Can you think of any other adjectives that may describe your family? Write them down in your journal or on your worksheet for future reference.

You could also write down in your journal *positive affirmations* about your family. Positive affirmations are things you say to yourself to remind you of your self-worth. For example, you may find it helpful to say to yourself—on days where you don't feel so good about yourself—something such as *My family is loving and will always support me*; *I have a strong family who pulls together when they really need to*; or *I am loved by my family and that will never change*.

In the next section, you will be able to identify the Black and mixed-race men and women who have contributed to your racial identity in powerful ways, to continue strengthening your sense of self-worth to protect yourself from emotional injury. In the end, you'll be able to see that there's worth and value in yourself, your family, and your cultural heritage.

ACTIVITY 4: KNOW YOUR HISTORICAL WORTH

This activity will allow you to explore the honorable Black and mixed-race historical figures who contributed to the development of our society in positive ways. You can find the worksheet to this activity at http://www.newharbinger.com/50126 or you can write down your answers in your journal.

Honorable Historical Leaders

Dr. Martin Luther King Jr.	James Baldwin
Francis Cecil Sumner	Ruby Bridges
Rosa Parks	Beverly Daniel Tatum
Shirley Chisholm	Joseph L. White
Sally Hemings	Herman George Canady
Inez Beverly Prosser	Octavius V. Catto
Kenneth Clark	Bessie Coleman
Mary Whiton Calkins	Mary Fields
Darrell "Bubba" Wallace Jr.	Rudolph Fisher
Mamie Phipps Clark	James Forten
Robert Lee Williams II	Francis Harper
Albert Sidney	Dorothy Height
Philippa Duke Schuyler	Nipsey Hussle
Kobi Kambon (Joseph A. Baldwin)	Benjamin Banneker
Maya Angelou	Cecil B. Moore
Frederick Douglass	Nina Simone
W.E.B. Du Bois	Sojourner Truth
Barack Obama	Henry T. Sampson
Muhammad Ali	Lewis Howard Latimer
Sadie Tanner Mossell Alexander	Keith Black

This activity is only a small picture of your historical worth. There's so much more to learn, and I encourage you to do further research on your history to continue understanding how worthy you are, and the legacy of strength you come from.

Moving Forward

We've done a lot of great and tough work in this chapter. You learned more about the relationship between thoughts, feelings, and behaviors that's central to CBT, and how cognitive distortions as well as negative self-talk can affect your level of confidence in yourself. You also learned two healthy coping skills—recognizing and changing negative self-talk, and recognizing and challenging cognitive distortions—that can help you separate yourself from the negative thoughts that racial trauma causes. And you've explored your racial identity, emotional injury, and your historical worth—all of which can be affected by racial trauma you've experienced *and* can also help you heal and protect yourself from racial trauma. Understanding who you are and your individual, family, and historical worth is an especially important step in healing from racial trauma. Knowing who you truly are—and how worthy you are of respect—reduces the negative self-talk that so easily invades your mind.

In the next chapter, you will dive deeper into the connection between thoughts, feelings, and behaviors by learning how to recognize the physical sensations, emotions, and behaviors within yourself that are caused by racial trauma, and what to do about them.

PART 2

Accepting and Healing
from Racial Trauma

CHAPTER 4

Coping with Racial Trauma Inside Your Body

Understanding your feelings can give you a cue to your thoughts, so you can continue working to change those if they're distorted or just not helpful. Some people have a hard time identifying their feelings and may not be able to fully understand what physical response or symptoms they are having until they really take the time to feel and understand them.

Having the proper coping skills can help you manage physical stress. These skills include techniques to get in touch with your body and calm and soothe yourself when you need to, especially when life gets tough and ways to build self-care and healthy behaviors into your routine.

Let's get started.

A Full-Body Experience

In the end, the experience of racial trauma is a full-body experience because it triggers the stress response and may cause you to think negatively about yourself. Once your stress response and negative self-talk are triggered—and you aren't able to calm down fast enough to recover from the stress response—you may begin to see worsening physical responses, like lack of energy, poor motivation, stomach aches, or headaches. You may also notice emotional responses such as sadness, isolation, and irritability. For example, if you are feeling depressed or anxious every day because of peers in school who do not understand that the way they casually use racial slurs, phrases, and idioms makes you feel left out or attacked, and it's clear you're one of the few Black or mixed-race people in that environment, your body may take a very long time to recover from this stress—even long after you leave school for the day. Or, if you find yourself worrying about your parent, who faces discrimination at work that stresses them out; you might carry this worry and stress with you, because this is a situation that neither you nor your parent can easily change. This prolonged physical response to stress can lead to wear and tear on the body and eventually cause a diagnosable condition such as depression, anxiety, or PTSD.

Note: If now or at any point, you feel like the symptoms you're having may be signs of depression, anxiety, or PTSD, turn to chapter 8 to learn more about these conditions and how to diagnose them.

In order to identify when the body is reacting to stress in your environment, an emotion you are having, or a negative thought that has crossed your mind, it is helpful to remember the relationship between thoughts, feelings, and behaviors, and to think about how the connection between these things can impact you. You can think of these three things as forming a CBT triangle. Let's look at the triangle Jasmine drew when she thought about her experience being bullied by the girls who threatened her.

Situation: I was bullied by a group of girls who don't like me.

Thoughts

What if this happens again?

Why are these girls always so mean?

Feelings

Fear, anger, stress, anxiety, sadness, shame

Behaviors

Not focusing in school, being excused

Crying in the bathroom at school

Avoiding things I used to do

Getting into fights at home

Next, you'll build on the work you have already done on negative self-talk by learning to connect your thoughts with the feelings and behaviors that typically come with them, and to help yourself identity negative or skewed thoughts that may prevent your healing.

ACTIVITY 5: CONNECT YOUR THOUGHTS, FEELINGS, AND BEHAVIORS

You'll find a worksheet for drawing your own triangle at http://www.newharbinger .com/50126.

Start by thinking of a situation that you are currently struggling with. For example, perhaps you are struggling with self-confidence because of negative thoughts you are having about your racial identity and how it's perceived. You will want to write this down as the situation. Next, you will write down the specific thoughts you are having about this situation. Then you will write down the emotions you feel because of the thoughts you are having. And lastly, you want to write down what you are doing in response—that is, what your behavior is—that may be making things worse for you. For example, perhaps you responded to this situation by isolating yourself in your room—and this isolation is making you feel worse about everything.

To give another example, say your school has a college counseling day. And perhaps, as you were thinking about everything you'll need to do to get your applications in, you thought, *I'll never make it through college because no one in my family did*. This thought may make you feel angry, sad, or ashamed, among other possible emotions. And these emotions, in turn, might lead you to struggle during the college counseling day, or at school in general. On the other hand, if you can recognize your thoughts, feelings, and behaviors, and understand the ways they're interacting with each other, you can learn ways to deal with what you're feeling and thinking. And you can stay on track with the college application process, even if it's hard.

These questions can help identify the connection between your thoughts, feelings, and behaviors.

Situation: What happened that triggered your stress response in the moment? Is it bothering you now?

Thoughts: Which thoughts came up for you in this situation?

Feelings:

When you experienced racism, what did you feel?

Did you feel helpless, hopeless, sad, or angry? Why?

Did you have mixed feelings? Do you know why?

Behaviors:

What did the thoughts or feelings you had about the situation lead you to do?

Did the emotion you felt in response to what was happening change how you reacted?

Did your behavior change because of what you were feeling or thinking?

It's always a healthy practice to examine what you are thinking, what you are feeling, and what you do—especially in response to an experience that's stressful or traumatic in some way. Knowing how you think, feel, and behave can help you identify helpful coping skills that are likely to help you in the long run.

Over the next week or so, try to watch for any moments when you feel especially stressed out. When you're in a moment like that, try to use what you've learned about negative self-talk and the CBT triangle to detect and separate the feelings you have, the thoughts that come with those feelings, and the behaviors that these feelings and thoughts lead you to do.

And see if doing this helps you think of some ways you might respond to the situation you're in and the stress you feel in a different way than you otherwise would.

Of course, it may be hard to do this in the moment, especially when you're first starting to try it. You can also try journaling, at the end of the day, about how you might have used what you've learned about the CBT triangle to do something differently than you actually did.

There may be times when you can't pinpoint how intense a specific emotion you are having is. Sometimes you may have many emotions at once. In such moments, using an emotions scale to rank how intense your emotions are may be helpful. You can try to identify each emotion you're feeling as best you can, and then rank each emotion using this scale.

1	2	3	4	5
barely feeling any emotion	feeling the emotion a little bit	feeling the emotion a lot	feeling the emotion very much	feeling the emotion extremely

One way I personally use the CBT triangle is by looking for evidence that contradicts how I may be feeling in the moment about something I am experiencing. For example, although I have quite a few years of therapy under my belt, there are times right before I meet with a new client that I feel a bit anxious. My immediate thought is something like *I hope I can help this person* or *I hope my style of therapy will be useful*. If I allow myself to think these thoughts and feel anxious without using any coping skills, my behavior may come across as disengaged or anxious. To avoid this happening, I focus on what matters most to me, which is helping people who come for treatment.

I also use positive affirmations to help counteract my negative thoughts and boost my confidence; for example, *Even though I may feel nervous now and I'm meeting this person for the first time, I have always been good with people and able to connect with them.* You could also remind yourself of a positive poem, inspirational message, or scripture.

The more you work with the CBT triangle, the more comfortable you'll be learning to understand your own thoughts, feelings, and behaviors—and doing so *before* any experiences of racism or family difficulty have become traumatic. One other protective thing that working with the CBT triangle in this way can help you learn to do is to figure out when to use coping activities—like the ones you'll learn about next—in the moments where you feel your thoughts are controlling you or creating tension in your life.

Mindfulness Meditation

One such coping activity is *mindfulness meditation*. Mindfulness meditation allows you to sit quietly and focus on calming your mind. It can be especially helpful if you sometimes find it difficult to figure out what you're feeling. After all, a lot of us don't often take the time to really feel our feelings. We may never have been taught how to connect with our feelings. And we may find it easier to wave them away or stuff them down, especially if they're painful. But often, if we can get in touch with our feelings, we can learn the valuable information they provide for us. And we can learn to process and deal with them, rather than letting them contribute to our stress and racial trauma.

Mindful Deep Breathing

Deep breathing can seem like an easy thing to do that doesn't require practice, but it is more than just taking long deep breaths. Deep breathing is an intentional practice that you can engage in when your body is feeling stressed and overwhelmed by racial trauma. It can also be useful in events where you feel you may have a panic attack or have trouble keeping yourself calm such as before a dance recital or sporting event. These steps can help you practice mindful deep breathing:

1. Find a place where you won't be interrupted, such as your room, the bathroom, or a quiet outdoor space Close your eyes and rest your hands near your sides. Breathe slowly and pay attention to how you are breathing.

2. Take a deep breath, allowing your abdomen to expand fully and your lungs to fill with air completely. (Try not to breathe just in your chest. That's where we often breathe when we're really stressed

or panicking. The abdomen is where we typically breathe when we're calm and relaxed—which is what we want to try to be.)

3. Notice what the air entering through your nose feels like as it fills your lungs. Notice your belly rise and fall as you breathe in and out.

4. Allow your breathing to be natural as air goes in through your nose and out through your mouth.

5. Breathe in and out two more times—allowing your breath to enter your lungs completely and leave your lungs completely. After the third full inhale and exhale, open your eyes.

Reflection: How do you feel after this activity? Are you feeling calmer and experiencing a relaxed body, free of tightness and stress?

I encourage you to use this mindful breathing as a form of self-care when you are feeling overwhelmed by your body's stress response. You can practice this exercise several times a day.

Mindful Meditation and Reflection

Another self-care activity that may be of help to you—especially when it comes to figuring out what you're feeling and thinking when those aren't quite clear—is mindful meditation and reflection.

Mindful meditation and reflection can be defined as a series of relaxing and focused thoughts to help you nurture your body and your mind. Mindful meditation and reflection can also be used to help you focus on the positive things you have in your life. Let's practice this activity.

1. Find a relaxing place to sit where you can have privacy and quiet. Begin by closing your eyes and inhaling, bringing your shoulders up, then exhaling and bringing your shoulders down, as a way to ground yourself. (*Grounding* is a technique that helps you focus on what you are seeing, feeling, or hearing in your immediate environment rather than paying attention to your anxiety, so that you can stay in control of your emotions. For example, if you are feeling like you might have a panic attack, grounding can help you focus on other things such as what you hear and see in your environment rather than your anxiety.) As you breathe in, pay attention to how the air is filling your nostrils and how the exhale is emptying out your lungs. Continue this breathing pattern for three complete breaths.

2. Allow your breathing to return to normal and gently tilt your head back and to the sides to stretch your neck. Continue to calmly breathe in and out as you stretch your neck for three complete breaths.

3. Relax your facial muscles, your shoulders, your arms, and your hands while continuing to breathe normally. Now move to relaxing your lower body as you breathe in and out calmly.

4. As you continue breathing, see what comes up in your mind. What are you feeling in your body? Are any thoughts or memories coming up? Do your best to just notice whatever arises, without acting on it. And without judging it as "good" or "bad," painful, shameful, or whatever else. (It will probably be hard to do this. Our minds are built to act on things and judge them. But the more you practice observing what comes up for you in this way, the easier it will get.

Over time, you may find this helps you understand what you're feeling and thinking and why—especially if it tends to be hard for you to figure out what you're feeling, or to separate your feelings from your thoughts.)

5. As an alternative, allow yourself to think of the positive things that happened today, or think about something that can make you smile. Continue to breathe as you allow your mind to think positive thoughts. Continue the positive thoughts for three complete breaths.

6. Once you complete your third breath (or at whatever point feels comfortable for you), open your eyes and allow your mind to return to the present moment. At this point you can grab your journal and begin writing down how you feel and why you feel that way after the meditation. Reflect on your experience during the meditation by writing down the thoughts that came into your mind and the emotions that you felt.

Reflecting on your experience during meditation can help you determine if this would be a helpful practice to continue using—either to get in touch with what you're thinking and feeling, or as part of processing an experience, even when it's tough, before it becomes trauma.

Note: If doing this or other techniques brings up particularly painful thoughts and feelings, you might want to turn to chapter 8 to see if you're experiencing diagnosable levels of depression, anxiety, or PTSD. That chapter will also guide you in how to pursue professional help, if you decide that's something you might need or want.

When we are most stressed and overwhelmed by what we and our families are facing, we can use mindfulness to practice self-care.

What Is Self-Care?

Self-care is a term that refers to activities you do to calm yourself and to help you regulate your emotions. When we practice self-care, we give our bodies time to recover from the stress response so that we can feel calm, focused, and strong within ourselves.

You might think that self-care is a little indulgent, or that it's time consuming and not necessary. But it's a crucial part of your health as a human being—and especially so when you are facing racism and other difficult experiences. So let's look at how to come up with a self-care plan.

A self-care plan is something that you can create on your own to help you manage the stress you may be having when it's at its strongest. A self-care plan doesn't include just things you like to do; rather, it includes activities and interests that truly rejuvenate your heart, soul, and mind and allow you to recover from stress.

The next activity will allow you to create your own self-care plan by figuring out what you want to do and when you want to do it.

ACTIVITY 6: CREATE YOUR SELF-CARE PLAN

A self-care plan is different from meeting your basic daily needs because you are actively choosing to help your body calm down when you are feeling overwhelmed. Self-care is an intentional practice that you engage in to directly affect the physical response your body is having to a stressful situation.

Below is a short list of tools you can use to reduce stress. I encourage you to add some of your own ideas to the list.

Acupuncture

Yoga

Karate or kung fu

Starting a journal that includes inspirational messages and positive art

Having a morning ritual that makes you feel connected and grounded

Turning off your cell phone and reading a good book or watching a good movie

Taking deep breaths

Being active: going to the gym, going on a hike, playing a sport

Stretching

Going to a support group or neighborhood gathering

Visiting with your neighbor

Baking something fun and delicious

Painting your nails

Doing art: painting, sketching, making a collage

Writing in your journal or in a journaling app

Going for a walk

Talking to someone who lifts you up: a therapist, a good friend, a spiritual advisor, a family member you trust

Eating a healthy snack

Trying a new food

Cooking a fun meal

Taking a calming bath, maybe with bath salts or soothing oils

Buying some flowers or plants to put in your room or space

Seeing a good movie

Planning your future in a journal

Learning how to play a musical instrument

Learning a new language

Listening to foreign music

Traveling to space with a guided imagery

Trying a relaxation app like Calm

Writing down all your favorite meals in a journal

Window shopping

Swimming or surfing

Once you've had a chance to consider the list, flip to a fresh page in your journal and write down all the activities you would find enjoyable to practice when feeling stressed. Do this in bullet-point format to keep yourself organized. Here's an example from my self-care plan.

- Doing an eye mask

- Doing a hair mask

- Doing a foot mask

- Watching a good documentary

- Going to bed early

- Exercising in the morning

Now, pick at least three self-care activities that you will use to keep yourself calm over the next week, and schedule those self-care activities in your week.

For example, when I set up my self-care plan, I decided I would go to bed by 10:00 p.m. from Monday through Thursday, exercise at 10:00 a.m. from Monday through Thursday, and have a fun family dinner on Saturdays. I also decided to use my foot masks, eye masks, and hair masks on Saturday afternoons, while I watch a documentary. When I honor my commitment to doing these self-care activities, I find they help me relax.

You will want to find ways to actually commit to the schedule you've laid out. I'm the kind of person who learns by visuals that are attractive and pretty. So if you learn best by using visuals as I do, I encourage you to use paper or a poster board, markers, glitter, stickers, and other materials to make your self-care plan something you want to look at and practice weekly. You can also put your self-care activities as reminders in your phone. Or you can get a friend to do some of your self-care activities with you to keep yourself accountable and have some fun.

Once you have all your self-care scheduled, see if you can realistically stick to your plan. If you have other activities that might get in the way, move your self-care activities to another day or another time. And if you find that an activity you thought would be doable and useful to you is actually less doable or less soothing that you thought it would be, swap in another activity that you *are* able to commit to and benefit from. You can always change your schedule so that you don't end up feeling like your self-care plan is a chore. A self-care list can be changed or altered at any time to meet your personal needs. In fact, I often encourage many of my teen clients to change their self-care list as they get older. I encourage you to do the same.

Also remember that you may not be able to practice self-care every day, and that's okay. Just try to come back to it again the next day. Over time, you'll likely find that scheduling your self-care activities into your day will help you feel better—especially on days when what you're feeling is hard to deal with.

Moving Forward

Racial trauma is something that may take a very long time to work through—but it isn't impossible. Once you understand the relationship between thoughts, feelings, and behaviors, you can work with that relationship to better understand what you're feeling and learn to process it, rather than just suffering. And the physical and emotional responses that you may be having to racism and racial trauma can be managed with self-care. Although you may struggle to find time for self-care activities, it's good to remember that you can't force yourself to just get over racial trauma. By using self-care to demonstrate faith in our body's ability to recover from racial trauma, we will begin to heal the wounds that racism has caused us.

In the next chapter, we will look at ways to overcome any fears that you may be experiencing because of racial trauma.

CHAPTER 5

Overcoming Your Fear

Fear is one of the toughest parts of dealing with racism and racial stress. It is a biochemical stress response triggered by a situation or memory that negatively affects you. It's important to understand that fear can change the way you see yourself, see others, and see the future. When you are gripped with fear on a constant basis—and influenced to avoid certain things in your life because of it—fear can imprison you and hold you hostage.

The only way to gain control of your fear response is to learn ways to manage it. In this chapter, we will look at how a special part of the brain reacts to fear—and then we will look at ways to overcome the fear that racial and family trauma can cause.

Your Brain's Fear Center

I used to struggle with fear as an adolescent. I was so unsure about who I was and whether people would accept or reject me as a Black and mixed-race teen. I never fully understood what was triggering the fear I felt, but I had a strong suspicion that a part of my brain was struggling with my reality of having to face a society so rejecting of my race. Growing up in a predominantly White neighborhood I was constantly experiencing justifiable fear.

As a Black or mixed-race teen, you may have learned that you can sense racism in any environment where it exists. You don't always need to see it or hear it clearly to experience the fear that it triggers. Internalized racism (your own beliefs about your race) and microaggressions can all trigger fear within you.

In fact, we have an interesting structure in the brain that "senses" the environment and reacts to the threat it perceives. There is an almond-sized structure in the middle of the brain, known as the *amygdala*. Though it is attached to a variety of other structures that contribute to our emotional responses, the amygdala itself plays a unique, important role in regulating our most powerful emotional responses. The amygdala can be thought of as the "house" of powerful emotions such as impulses, aggression, and reactive behavior.

When you are faced with any kind of racial trauma—bullying, harassment, threats, or assaults—your amygdala quickly examines the situation and responds to the threat. The amygdala does not think things through or examine the pros and cons of the situation. It just reacts. This means your amygdala is responsible for reactions you may have in response to a negative situation, such as fear and anxiety. Negative situations are ones that our brains perceive as threats. And when we're faced with threats, we don't stop to really think about them. We simply act.

Another important function of the amygdala is to give meaning—emotional meaning—to our experiences. Recall from chapter 2 that Jasmine wanted to avoid the cafeteria because of what happened the day she was assaulted by peers on her way home. Walking by the cafeteria would trigger her amygdala to remember the experience and cause a fear response. Jasmine knew a fear response would include a panic attack, sweating, feeling afraid, and wanting to escape.

Refection: Can you think of an experience like this that you may have had? Can you recall a time when you experienced fear that was triggered in this way?

When your brain makes the association between these negative experiences and your emotions, a fear response is triggered. You may begin to experience nervousness that can take many different forms and have varying levels of intensity, including even panic attacks. For example, some people experience increased heartrate and sweating, while others may only experience fidgeting and racing thoughts.

Fear Is Not Always Bad

One important lesson my mother taught me was that fear can be good—it is a warning signal that we may need to be protected from something in our environment at the time. Fear helps us scan our environment for things that could potentially harm us and prepare for things we might need to protect ourselves against, so it's okay to feel fearful when you are facing an uncomfortable experience. The fear response is there to protect and alert you to danger—and this is true even if the danger isn't exactly tangible.

Fear can also help you learn to understand why you feel what you feel. With practice, you can learn to distinguish when fear is helpful and when it's not, as well as what you can do to respond to fear (or anything else) consciously rather than automatically.

You can overcome fear by using the correct tools and finding coping skills that are useful to you. So now that you understand the fear response and where it originates, let's look at ways to overcome this fear response.

How the Brain Responds to Fear

The brain is a complex organ that has a lot of jobs to perform. Any fear reaction or traumatic experience can throw it off course. Recall from chapter 2 how the body responds to a threat like a gas pedal that speeds up, with a brake pedal that slows things down when the threat is gone. But the brain is also resilient—meaning it can change depending on what it experiences, and so, with the right tools and the right approach, it can heal itself. In other words, even though you have experienced racial trauma, your brain still has the capacity to heal—to unlearn the patterns it's been taught in the past and learn new patterns, patterns that can make you calmer, more resilient, and more secure in your surroundings and your self-worth in the long run. That's what makes the brain so complex and so very interesting.

When you feel afraid, the body's central nervous system speeds up like an engine. One way you can turn off the engine and begin healing the brain is by doing calming activities, like the mindfulness or self-care practices you explored last chapter, any time you feel afraid. The more committed you are to using calming activities, the more resilient your brain will become. Consider your brain to be like a rubber band. The more you allow fear to stretch your brain, the harder it becomes for it to regain its original shape. Strengthening your resilience to help heal the brain from trauma involves using techniques to prevent the brain from being stretched by fear.

Let's move into looking at the kinds of fear response you have experienced and how you have responded to help you identify similar reactions to fear when they arise in the future.

Identify Your Fear Response and Challenge Distortions

It's normal to experience fear and for your brain and body to react to it by triggering the stress response discussed in chapter 1. In this activity you will reflect on what causes your fear response, the specific bodily sensations and thoughts that arise when your fear response is triggered, and how to respond to those thoughts, in particular, using your knowledge of cognitive distortions. This will help you adjust your behavior—the ways you act when your fear response is triggered.

ACTIVITY 7: IDENTIFY YOUR FEAR

Let's begin by exploring what fear feels like for you. I encourage you to use your journal to help you reflect on the questions that follow or to download the worksheet at http://www.newharbinger.com/50126. I will also give you an example from my own life to help you practice this activity.

What are some things that cause you to feel afraid?

What do you notice when you are feeling afraid? Do you experience body changes such as an increased heart rate, sweating, or fidgeting?

What emotions come up for you when you are feeling afraid, such as a feeling of not being able to get through the moment?

Is there a specific situation that might trigger you to feel fear?

How does your body react to fear when you are afraid of something? Do you notice your muscles feeling tight, anxiety, a feeling of helplessness, or anger?

What thoughts typically arise when you are afraid?

Which, if any, cognitive distortions do you experience when you are afraid?

Sometimes it is helpful to identify people (or things) that can help you work through your fears so that when you experience fear again, you will know what to do to help you cope better. For example, let's say you are struggling with going to school every day because of fear that your teacher doesn't like you because of the color of your skin. Who can you rely on to help you through this situation? Is there anyone who can make you feel safe and loved? Who in your life accepts you just the way you are? Is it your mom or dad? A trusted teacher? The school principal?

Let me now share my experience with you to give you another example of how to identify your fears and cognitive distortions. One thing that made me afraid in the past was having to speak before a large audience. I was invited to speak at a national conference as a keynote speaker on racism and discrimination. I knew a lot was expected of me—and I highly respected the invitation. At the same time, as I thought about having to speak, I could feel my usual fear response coming on. As a woman of color, I feared that I would not be able to relate to my audience in the ways I felt I had to.

I decided to use one of my coping skills for this—journaling, writing down what I was feeling and thinking to try to understand what I felt and why. And as I journaled about how anxious I was, I realized that what made me afraid was public speaking on a difficult topic, feeling that I might be misjudged as a woman of color. I had two cognitive distortions, in particular, that were causing a lot of anxiety. One was minimization: an instinct to minimize both my gift of speaking, which I know I have, and the faith everyone had in me to give a good speech. The other was emotional reasoning: believing I would fail because of how afraid I felt in the moment, when in reality there was no guarantee that whatever fear I felt would ensure I'd fail.

Once I became aware of all this, I realized I had other coping skills I could use to deal with what I was feeling in a better way than just staying stuck in my fear response. Right before I went on stage, I had eight minutes to take some mindful deep breaths (discussed in chapter 4) and refocus my attention. I remember feeling afraid of what could happen and feeling my mind beginning to wander into negative thoughts. But now that I knew the distortions that powered my fearful thoughts, I could immediately question my negative thoughts by asking myself these questions, which brought my attention back to the reality of my situation.

Why am I so anxious about getting on stage?

How do I know I will fail?

What if I succeed and truly help my audience feel better about who they are?

What strengths do I have right now that I can rely on to help me through this moment?

Reflection: Can you think of an experience where your fear caused you to doubt yourself?

Again, it's okay to feel afraid and it's okay to give into your fears sometimes. But the goal is always to overcome your fear, so it is important to learn healthy ways of managing your fears rather than avoiding them.

Thought Stopping

Another way to manage your fears—especially when you're dealing with tough thoughts and you don't really have the time to journal or explore cognitive distortions in depth—is by using a technique called *thought stopping.*

The idea behind thought stopping is that you can take an unwanted or negative thought and completely shut it off by not thinking about it. For example, if Jasmine expects to see her bullies at school and begins to have thoughts like *They are going to beat me up* or *They'll ignore me if they see me,* she can intentionally shift her attention to another thought: a positive message she read this week, her upcoming birthday party, or the summer vacation spot she is waiting to go to.

Stopping a distressing thought gives you control and allows you to choose another topic for your mind to focus on in the moment. You also allow yourself to feel better about the possibilities.

The best way to practice the thought-stopping technique is by using it every time you experience a negative thought. You can use the acronym ADS—*acknowledge, determine,* and *substitute*—to help you remember the three steps of thought stopping.

When you have a negative thought, pause and

1. **Acknowledge** the unwanted thought you are having (for example, *No one will ever accept me in my school because of my skin color*).

2. **Determine** what coping skill would be helpful to you in that moment (for example, squeezing an ice cube, telling yourself to stop aloud, closing your eyes and breathing deeply for one whole minute, snapping a rubber band against your wrist, or verbalizing the thought out loud).

3. **Substitute** the negative thought with a balanced or positive thought (for example, *Some kids may not accept me but that doesn't mean all the kids in my school won't*).

This technique works for some people but not others. To give you enough time to determine if it will work for you, I encourage you to practice thought stopping for at least one to two weeks before you decide whether you'll keep using it.

It's also worth noting that while thought stopping does involve interrupting the sequence of a negative thought and switching to a positive one, the point of thought stopping isn't to suppress negative thoughts or stuff them down. And it isn't to deny that things are hard or that the unwanted thoughts you have aren't painful or don't have some truth to them. The point is to help you learn to pause in moments when you feel you're encountering racism or are on the verge of a trauma response, assess the situation realistically, and look for helpful ways to respond to the situation and the fear or stress you feel. You can also always use techniques like journaling or self-care strategies like talking to a friend or a trusted adult when you have negative thoughts, feelings, and experiences that you think you need to process on a deeper level than a technique like thought stopping might allow.

Let's look at Jasmine's story about stopping negative thoughts.

I have always had negative thoughts—about how other people see me, about how hard things will be, about how things will turn out for me. It's like I was born to think negatively. Sometimes my mom calls me Negative Nancy, and my dad asks if I am ever satisfied with anything. They just don't get it. I can't help the way I think! If I could change it, I would. My thoughts just pop up in my head when I least expect it, and sometimes I don't even know it is happening. Sometimes I feel like I have questions for everything, and I always look at the downside of things, especially with school. I got a B- in my favorite class, biology, the other day, and I beat myself up for days: How are you so bad in your favorite class? You're stupid, you have to be. In my eyes, I was a failure.

Reflection: What are Jasmine's negative thoughts? Do they fit with what you know about her and what she's capable of? How might you use *ADS* to help Jasmine change her negative thoughts into balanced thoughts?

But when my therapist taught me thought stopping—how to catch a negative thought before it goes too far, and choose to change it—it really helped. When I wake up for school in the morning, the first thought I have is Why do I have to get up? I hate seeing people at school. Before this thought comes into my mind again, I start thinking about my friends and how fun it will be to see them at lunch. When I'm having repeated anxious thoughts about the girls who bullied me, I'm able to stop, acknowledge the thought, and then tell myself: You're ruminating. And then I can use one of my coping skills, like taking a deep breath so I can bring myself back to reality and figure out how I want to approach the situation. Like yesterday, even when I saw those girls in the hall and felt fear coming on, I told myself: You don't have to let these girls intimidate you and control your life. You don't need to be afraid of them. And I decided to act normal. And it worked. They did look at me. But I think they finally realized I don't have to fear them. They didn't say anything to me.

Another longer-term way to cope with fear is to create a wellness plan.

Wellness Plans for Long-Term Coping

A wellness plan is like any plan of action—it's a way to come up with specific steps that you put together to achieve a goal. In this case, your ultimate goal is to overcome fear and develop new skills to help you cope better. A wellness plan will help you set specific goals and break them down into smaller steps so that it will be easier to achieve. It's distinct from the self-care plan you came up with in chapter 4—a self-care plan is about the specific purpose of self-care, which is one aspect of wellness; the wellness plan is a bigger, longer-term investment in yourself and your life so that you can develop better habits over time. Like the self-care plan, it becomes part of you and is built into your life. The self-care and wellness plans are both important to helping you build and maintain healthy coping skills when life is toughest.

Creating a wellness plan is an opportunity to look at what it means to you to live a good life that makes you and the people you love happy and fulfilled. It's a chance to consider how you can work to build yourself the life that you, like everyone, deserve no matter what your experiences with racism and racial trauma may sometimes lead you to believe. And it's an opportunity to try new things, practice new behaviors, and adopt new skills into your life daily or weekly.

ACTIVITY 8: CREATE YOUR WELLNESS PLAN

Your wellness plan is a plan for you to take care of yourself in positive ways in many different areas. It's very important to take care of yourself so that you will be prepared for how your body may react to fear. Trying to change old patterns of behavior—being attentive to your overall wellness—can feel overwhelming. But once you map out your wellness plan—the specific actions you'll take in a variety of life domains to live a good life—and practice the activities you've identified every day, you may find this process a lot easier than you thought.

Let's look at an example of what a wellness plan may look like. At http://www.newhar binger.com/50126, you'll find blank copy of this wellness worksheet to complete on your own.

Category	What I'll Do	When I'll Do It
Physical health	Exercise at the gym with my mom	Tuesdays, Thursdays, and Saturdays
Diet	Eat more leafy greens such as salads and kale	At least four days a week at dinner time
Sleep	Turn off screens an hour before I go to bed	Seven days a week
Emotional health	Attend therapy and see my school counselor	Weekends to talk to my therapist, twice a week for my school counselor
Environmental health	Volunteer to plant new flowers at the senior citizen facility and other community sites	On Saturdays and Sundays for as long as they need it
Spiritual health	Go to youth group at my church	Every Wednesday night
Psychological health	Talk to my pastor about the feelings I have	Next Sunday after church
Intellectual health	Read five good books on a topic new to me	During my summer vacation
Your vision for the future	Write down five careers or jobs I might like and do some research on them	Research one career or job every Saturday or Sunday until I find one I like

Your vision for the future is a special category that represents the things you want to achieve in your life. It prepares you to plan and commit to certain actions that will help you make those dreams real. And it allows you to remember the reality that you have a life beyond racism and racial trauma, and that life is worth living.

Which categories in this list are ones you know you want to work on? On your own worksheet, check off those categories. There may also be categories that you know you should be working on but don't feel very inspired by; put a second check next to those.

Next you can begin to create a plan for how you will include each category you've checked into your schedule. For example, let's say you want to address the categories of diet and psychological health. One way to start is by listing—on paper or in your journal—how you will improve these categories in your life.

For some categories, you might want to work on whatever actions you plan to take every day, rather than every week. Or, if you have a longer-term goal, you might find it better to consider how many times a month you want to work toward the goal in question. In the end, the most important step in creating your wellness plan is staying true to yourself and only writing down things you know you will commit to practicing.

If you're struggling to identify categories at all, keep reading. In the rest of this chapter, we'll explore what it means to work on these different categories of health and wellness, and this discussion may help clarify some things for you.

Emotion Regulation Techniques

Another important part of your wellness plan is thinking of ways to help yourself regulate your emotions when you feel triggered by something such as a racial slur or a rude comment. When you are feeling overwhelmed by your thoughts and feelings and are unable to focus on anything in your immediate environment, emotion regulation techniques are very helpful.

To be successful in your healing process, you have to learn a bit about the techniques available to you. These techniques include:

- relaxing, for example by spending time with animals, spending time in a beautiful garden, painting or drawing, or cooking;

- mindfulness meditation, such as listening to a guided imagery or sitting quietly to think about your experiences;

- · self-awareness by journaling, writing poetry, or listening to music that causes you to think;

- self-care, such as exercising, eating healthy, going to bed earlier or waking up earlier, and writing down positive affirmations;

- self-compassion, by showing yourself the same amount of care and concern that you would show someone you care about;

- self-soothing, such as having a spa day or washing your hair with your favorite shampoo.

These activities all target our gas and brake pedal systems, as was discussed in chapter 2.

Now that you have started your wellness plan and included the categories you might like to focus on, let's explore what it's going to take to maintain good emotional and psychological health—two of the most important categories of wellness, and the ones that can be most affected by racial trauma. You can think of psychological health as involving your thoughts and how you perceive your experiences. Your emotional health involves focusing on reducing stress and controlling your emotions.

Working on Your Psychological and Emotional Health

When you've experienced trauma, it is important for you to focus on rebuilding your psychological self from the inside out, using tools like self-reflection to understand your feelings and thoughts, and knowing how to uncover the kinds of distortions in your thinking that racial trauma can create. Taking care of yourself means empowering yourself through knowledge, encouragement, and self-help. You may feel so discouraged by what you are going through that you don't want to put effort into feeling better. But if you put one foot in front of the other, have a plan, and test that plan daily, you may find that you can take care of yourself much better than you thought.

And whether the racial trauma in your life has been direct (that is, you experienced the racism) or indirect (like in the case of intergenerational trauma), it is important to find ways to stay balanced and positive. Your emotional health is just as important as your psychological health. You can work on your emotional health by continuing to practice the coping skills you've learned in previous chapters:

- mindfully observing your internal experience so you can understand it *before* your stress response or automatic behavior kicks in;

- using your knowledge of the CBT triangle to figure out what you're feeling when things get hard, what kinds of thoughts those feelings are fueling, and how those thoughts and feelings are driving you to behave;

- using self-awareness practices like journaling to continue building your skills of processing experiences before they have a chance to cause the emotional chaos they might otherwise cause.

Let's also talk about a few more ways you can stay connected to the people and things that can help you cope with trauma—a way to build your psychological and emotional resources when things get hard.

Ground yourself: Grounding is a technique, somewhat similar to mindfulness meditation, that you can use when you feel that stress and tension are overwhelming you. Grounding exercises include sitting still and focusing on the things that you hear, see, and feel on your skin. For example, you can sit quietly at a park and focus on the sounds all around you—naming aloud or in your head what you hear—so that your attention narrows to that thing you hear. You can also name the things you see. Grounding is a helpful way to focus your attention when you feel scattered.

Connect with family and friends: Staying connected to the people you trust and love is important for maintaining your emotional and psychological health. When you experience trauma, you may also experience feeling detached from people in your life. It's almost as if you become numb to things around you. Staying close to family and friends is one way to maintain your overall health.

Make a list of things that make you happy: Sometimes you may need to be reminded that life isn't all bad. Making a list of all the things that make you happy and keeping it in your room or somewhere you can see it often can make all the difference in your maintaining your emotional and psychological health.

Embrace art and music: Art and music are really useful for managing negative thoughts and feelings because they allow you to express your deepest emotions and feel connected to something bigger than your fears. Many research studies done on victims of trauma suggest that these areas (as well as other forms of self-expression, like poetry and theater) all contribute to the well-being and healing of the person. Creative expression also stimulates the emotional centers of the brain such as the amygdala so that we can make new memories and recover from traumatic experience. Try to experiment with some forms of artistic expression and see what feels good to you. This particular step can also feed into the spiritual and intellectual domains of your self-care plan.

Practice prayer/meditation/reflection: Using spiritual coping and staying connected to your spiritual side can be a great coping skill. Meditation, prayer, and sitting silent so that you can reflect on your thoughts and feelings can be helpful when you feel scattered. If you feel scattered you may notice symptoms such as trouble paying attention for long periods of time, boredom, confusion, and the presence of many thoughts in your mind. Sitting still and taking some time for yourself can help reduce feeling scattered. Another way to engage in emotion regulation techniques is by taking care of your overall health by getting eight to ten hours of sleep at night, taking care of your hygiene, and following a routine every day. You may want to try reading, journaling, or meditating in the morning when you wake up; spending quality time with positive and supportive people; exercising or going to the gym during the week for some "me time"; reading books, articles, and magazines on self-improvement; connecting with other young people seeking support in the community and meeting for lunch; and having a relaxation routine every night before bed (for example, taking a warm shower or bubble bath, listening to calming music).

Get into a support group: Support groups for teens can really help you feel at home and safe. If you would like to see how other teens are coping with racial trauma and feel supported by people your age, a support group may be a good option.

Get into coaching: Coaching is different from psychotherapy. Coaching focuses on helping you reach your goals. For example, say that one of your visions for the future is to build resilience so you can get into college in the next nine months. A coach who is experienced in helping clients meet their goals one step at a time can help you map out the exact steps to accomplish this goal and then take them.

Practice self-advocacy: Standing up for yourself may include creating your own support group at school, getting on a discussion panel on politics or racial segregation, volunteering your time, becoming a peer support for teens at your school, or writing articles or blogs on the topic of race—anything you do to get your own needs met and build a positive relationship with your own racial identity.

Limit your exposure to racialized news as needed: Sometimes the news and the things you may see on TV can impact your mood in a negative way. Sometimes it is best to just turn off the media and take a break from it.

Although healing racial trauma can take some time, it isn't impossible to overcome. You just need the right tools and the right approach so that you can heal and become a better you.

Sometimes it may be difficult for you to think about what your life would be like if you didn't have to experience racism. Racism can cause you to feel unmotivated, sad, and afraid. If you experience these emotions for too long without using healthy coping skills or thinking about positive things in your life, you can begin to believe that your future will also be negative.

ACTIVITY 9: YOUR NEW STORY

At http://www.newharbinger.com/50126 you can download a worksheet with these prompts, which will help you describe positive things that you would like to have in your future. You can also use your journal.

Prompt 1: Using words or drawing, describe some of the positive things you would like to do in your future. For example, you may want to learn how to drive and get your license before you turn eighteen. Or you may want to get all As this school year.

Prompt 2: Write down three positive goals that you can set for yourself to accomplish now. For example, you may want to join a sports team at another school or try out at your own school to become a cheerleader this year.

Prompt 3: Write down three talents or skills you could improve upon over the next six months.

Prompt 4: If you had a magic wand and could change anything about yourself right now what would that be?

Your wellness plan can also be used to help you design a new course of action for your life. Healing from trauma also includes looking ahead to your future and setting new goals for yourself. Let's see how Jasmine identifies long-term life goals for herself and takes steps to achieve them.

I have been feeling a lot better since learning new ways to heal from trauma. I really like my wellness plan and some of the things I have learned I can do when I'm not feeling too positive about things. It's great to have a plan in place and goals that I can remind myself of.

My first goal is to heal from trauma by learning new skills to help myself when things get tough. To do this I will reach out to my church or pastor—by email or phone—and ask if I can join the youth group there. I will also ask my mom if I could go to therapy to talk to someone about how I feel.

My second goal is to graduate from high school with good grades and a plan to go to college by getting all my work done on time, turning it in, and talking with my academic advisor at least once a month. I will practice prayer/meditation/reflection when I start to feel overwhelmed or upset so that I can keep studying and turning my work in on time.

My third goal is to go to college or get a job and not feel ashamed of who I am because of being bullied in school. I will talk openly with my coach and pastor when I start to doubt my abilities. I can also stay connected to the people who support me, such as my family, friends, and those in my church.

As you can see from this example, Jasmine has used her wellness plan to help her set new, achievable goals.

Healing from any kind of emotional injury or trauma doesn't just happen overnight. You must work at it. And healing from a systemic harm like racism also requires that you focus on *holistic healing*. Holistic healing means focusing on all parts of who you are—your mind, body, and soul. Focusing on only one part of who you are can short-circuit your progress. One you begin the process of healing your trauma you can then set healthy new goals that are realistic and practical to your daily life. Having a clear path will help you feel inspired along the way.

Moving Forward

Now that you have explored the stresses and fears you have experienced because of racism, learned coping skills to manage those fears, and begun thinking about building yourself routines to stay well and keep yourself protected against the harms of racism, you can begin to break the cycle of trauma in your family—starting with you. In the next chapter, we will look at the ways that racism can cause your family to compare itself to other families, get stuck in unhealthy cycles, and suffer from long-term grief and loss—and what you can do to stop it.

CHAPTER 6

Breaking the Cycle

Trauma creates cycles in your life and your family's life. Intergenerational cycles—cycles that repeatedly happen in your family—can be stopped, but only if you take the initiative in your own healing process.

Cycles and Comparisons

You may notice cycles in your family such as negative traditions, likes and dislikes, beliefs, behaviors and attitudes, and coping styles. You may also notice your own negative cycles such as procrastination, low self-esteem, lack of confidence, and fear.

For example, as a result of how they have been treated because of racism, some families may struggle with years of negative beliefs about themselves and others that keep them feeling discouraged or unable to accomplish things in life. They may also believe that because no one in the family ever went to college, you too may not go to college or have financial stability so that you can live a happy life. And your family may also have the belief that Black or mixed-race people will never be accepted in society no matter how hard they work to achieve certain goals.

These beliefs can end up influencing the ways you think and feel. For instance, if most of your family did not go on to college or complete college, it may cause you to believe that you too will not complete college—which may not be true. If your family has experienced difficulty achieving financial stability, it may cause you to believe that you too will never be financially stable—another belief that may not be true. If your family has experienced a difficult situation like the incarceration of a family member, or mental health crises in the family that didn't get treated as they should have, or living in an area that's under-resourced or overpoliced, you may end up with a belief that things will always be hard and never change—yet another belief that may not be true. These kinds of beliefs can be passed on for many generations within your family and cause you to give up rather than push forward through challenges you may face.

That's another thing that can be passed on for many generations—the behavior of giving up and the attitude that things will never change. When a family that already struggles with these beliefs, attitudes, and behaviors then experiences further racism, these beliefs, attitudes, and behaviors become reinforced—they become stronger in the family and may negatively impact future generations. This is how the cycle of intergenerational trauma gets started in families and how it persists.

Breaking the cycle of trauma, low self-esteem, depression, and anxiety involves identifying the negative thoughts, feelings, and behaviors that keeps the unhealthy cycle going, and doing your best to work with the negative thoughts and feelings so they don't influence your behavior as they otherwise might.

For example, if you recall from chapter 2, Jasmine noticed the cycle of racism in her family—the way that the experiences of being excluded and marginalized as Black people had repeated themselves in her grandmother's life and her mother's life—and saw that the same thing was happening to her. Jasmine saw that both her mother and grandmother experienced a lot of emotional pain because of refusing to acknowledge their own racial trauma, instead internalizing racism and refusing to talk about it. It wasn't necessarily their fault. Jasmine understood that experiencing racism had been painful for them, and that people don't always want to talk about the things that are painful. Sometimes it's enough to just have to deal with it. But she could also see the same pattern at work in her own life: the pattern of having hard experiences of racism, mistreatment, and being devalued, and not talking about it or working through it, so that it ended up steering what she felt and thought, what she was able to do, and how she felt about herself. She chose to break that cycle by taking the initiative to learn about herself and reach out for support.

The best way you can break the cycles in your life is if you are willing to explore these cycles and then change them. Jasmine saw how difficult things were for her mother and grandmother and did not want to experience this herself. She also recognized that, in the long run, avoiding the hard work of breaking this cycle of trauma would not help her heal from her own racial trauma that came from experiences like being bullied by girls at school and letting them control her sense of self-worth.

Another powerful cycle that can affect Black and mixed-race people who experience racism is that of comparisons. Comparisons of skin color, accent or tone of voice, hair texture or style, fashion, and financial status can happen a lot because of the frequent reminders from our society that the Black community is seen as having little value. Racial trauma has a lot to do with the way Black and mixed-race people see themselves in a society where one culture is highly valued over another. Comparing yourself to others can become a natural response to racism and lead to the feeling that Black people are marginalized, oppressed, and devalued. In many cases, you may not even recognize that you are comparing yourself to someone else and that these comparisons are driving you to feel and think in particular ways. This is often how a cycle begins.

Why You Compare Yourself to Others

For the most part you may feel like you have decent self-esteem and appreciate certain things about yourself, but there may be days when you feel like you have nothing to offer.

As a Black or mixed-race person, you may feel that it's impossible to find a reason to be confident about who you are. You may feel like there are no positive examples of people around you or on TV and online who look like you. You may feel like you are the only person in your school who looks like you. You may even overhear a peer talking about how different you are in school. Or you may feel like the people around you have it much easier than you and your family does, because they don't have to deal with the same racist systems and traumas that you and your family deal with.

As you explore your racial identity, you may notice cycles that you engage in when you are feeling less confident about yourself, especially when you compare yourself to people who don't seem to be struggling with what you struggle with. These cycles may include negative self-talk, shutting down and refusing to engage with others, being shy and hiding parts of yourself from others to avoid being judged, and taking the quiet role so you will go unnoticed. And these patterns of unhealthy behavior can make it hard for you to heal from racial trauma and do the things you really want to do: live the free, confident, happy life that you, like everyone else, deserve to live.

Know that it's okay to feel this way from time to time. Everyone feels this way at some point in their lives. And know that despite everything your mind may be telling you in these moments, you still have so much to offer to other people. You just have to find that confidence within yourself and learn to be okay with who you are.

Growing up, I had few positive examples of Black and mixed-race girls or boys my age. Most television shows—including popular stations for kids—all included girls and boys who were White. Everywhere I turned for positive reinforcement of my race I found nothing and no one who looked like me.

It wasn't until I engaged in self-reflection and really learned about who I was that I recognized the cycle of comparing myself to others. It was reflecting upon my own thoughts and feelings—and openly discussing them with people I trusted—that helped me overcome this cycle. At that point, I refused to continue comparing myself to others as though it were a fact that I was less worthy than they were. And I came to understand that the reasons I didn't see many people like me either in my neighborhood or in popular culture were systemic ones.

It wasn't just because *I* was different. It was because I lived in a society in which people of different races are typically segregated—not legally, but in practice, because of historical disparities and differences in who can access what. And it was because in our society, people are encouraged to stereotype and marginalize each other, thanks to the messages we all receive about who's worthy and who's not. This cycle of oppression and racism that we experience has a way of seeping into the minds of even young children—causing them to doubt who they are and who they can become as they grow up.

Thankfully I found my way out of this cycle with many of the tips I've shared with you here and many more that have become significant to my life's journey. And I learned, over the years and through many experiences, that appreciating who you are comes a lot easier when you finally decide that there is only one you—and there is great value in you when you allow yourself to be who you truly are.

To change how you think about yourself in comparison to others, it may be helpful to reflect upon your thoughts and feelings about who you are and who your family is, and how those thoughts and feelings might have been influenced by experiences of racism you've had.

ACTIVITY 10: YOUR CYCLE OF COMPARISONS

In this activity, you will be able to reflect on your thoughts and feelings using the prompts listed below. You can find the worksheet for this activity online at http://www .newharbinger.com/50126.

Do I compare myself to others my age? Why?

Do I compare my family to other families? Why?

Do I compare my race to others who are like me? Why?

Do I compare my race to others who are not like me? Why?

Is the first thought that comes to my mind about my race negative or positive?

Do I recognize my own self-worth or the worth of my family? If not, why am I unable to see this?

Do I feel stressed when I think others may be better than me? What do I feel in my body? What do I think?

How much time in total do I spend comparing myself to others during the week?

What thoughts am I having that are causing me to compare myself to others?

What are the feelings causing me to compare myself to others?

Once I've compared myself or my family to others, how do I feel? What are the specific emotions I feel?

Do I ever feel better when I compare myself to others? If not, why? If I do feel better, why?

You may feel that it will be difficult to break this cycle in your life—especially if you have compared yourself a lot in the past to others. But don't give up. There are ways to break these cycles, such as by using your coping skills (for example, journaling how you feel or doing a brief meditation), writing down your goals, or having a wellness plan and sticking to it. Let's start by looking at how you may be creating these cycles in your life.

Creating Negative Cycles

The thoughts you wrote about in the previous activity may have been varied and complex. But ultimately, CBT teaches us that a lot of our thoughts, emotions, and behaviors follow the same basic pattern. You can think of this pattern as the ABCs of thinking. First, there's an **activating event** (what happened), which could be anything you encounter that has triggered you to feel an intense emotion. For Black and mixed-race people, hearing about racism on the news may be a trigger for feelings of anger, hurt, or sorrow. Shortly after the activating event has taken place, the **belief** (the acceptance that something is true) about what happened occurs. After the belief comes the **consequence** (what happens because of the belief). The consequence may be anger, sadness, and fear. The consequence could also be comparing yourself to someone you think is better than you because of their race. After hearing about Jasmine's experience of being bullied in school because of her race (activating event), her grandmother and mother began to re-experience the negative thoughts about themselves that had negatively impacted their family for generations. Jasmine's mother and grandmother began to believe, *We will never be fully accepted as Black or mixed-race people.* Another belief was, *We will never break this cycle of trauma in our family.* The consequence of these beliefs included Jasmine's grandmother and mother both feeling discouraged and angry as a Black and mixed-race family who experienced racial trauma long ago. Her mother began to relive her own experience of being bullied and singled out because of her race.

When Jasmine talked to her therapist about the bullying incident that had caused her PTSD, her therapist suggested that they apply the ABC model to what she had experienced. Together, they determined that being pushed against the wall and threatened was the activating event or trigger Jasmine had experienced. And they worked through the beliefs that this activating event had caused or reinforced for Jasmine. For example, Jasmine began to believe that she couldn't stand up for herself or tell anyone about the bullying for fear that the bullying would get worse. One belief was *These girls will always bully me.* Another was *Something might happen to me at school at any time. I won't be able to control it.* A third was *There's no one at school who can support me. I'm like the only Black person there.* And then they considered the consequences of these beliefs. One was that Jasmine felt anxious and angry in ways she couldn't always control. She would lash out sometimes at school or at home. Another consequence was that she felt afraid of being bullied again and intimidated. She also began to question if she would ever be accepted by people who didn't look like her.

As you can see from Jasmine's experience, it can be hard to stop this ABC cycle once it gets started. The only way to manage this cycle is to (1) understand how it is operating in your life; (2) recognize that different activating events in your life often lead to negative beliefs; (3) learn to question those beliefs, using reflection questions like the ones earlier in this book; (4) practice replacing the thoughts you typically have with more helpful or accurate thoughts; and (5) let those thoughts bring you to new behaviors, different from the stress- and fear-driven ones you might otherwise rely on, along with using coping skills like meditation, journaling, and more to build your resilience generally.

When Jasmine did this with her therapist, they worked to challenge the beliefs that being bullied had left her with. For example, was it true that if something happened to Jasmine at school, she wouldn't be able to control it? Was it true that she would never be able to enjoy her life because of her race? Was it true that she would never be accepted by other people because of her race?

They also determined that the belief *There's no one at school who can support me* wasn't entirely true. Yes, there weren't many other Black or mixed-race kids at her school who would fully understand the experience she'd had. And yes, talking to her teachers was sometimes uncomfortable. But she had a few close friends there she liked talking to, and she could try leaning on them when she needed to. As you learned from Jasmine's ecomap in chapter 2, she was afraid her friends wouldn't understand her experience of racism. But this, her therapist pointed out, was an assumption—a distorted thought. Perhaps she could reframe or fix that assumption to help her better cope with the situation. She didn't have real evidence it was actually true. She realized, with the help of her therapist, that she was using emotional reasoning and fortune telling—another distorted thought you learned from chapter 3. What she needed to do was to try reaching out to her friends to see what would actually happen.

Jasmine and her therapist also brainstormed ways she could prevent the activating event—being bullied by that group of girls—from happening again. One was to use thought stopping to resist the instinct to be intimidated by the girls when they gave her harsh looks in the halls at school. As you learned in chapter 5, Jasmine ended up using that strategy, and it worked!

Jasmine and her therapist also decided that she would let at least one person at school she felt she could trust know about the incident so she had some support in case the girls did harass her again. After all, it wouldn't be fair to expect Jasmine to deal with their racist and violent behavior all on her own. So they decided that Jasmine would tell the school nurse and school counselor about what had happened to her and why she kept having to come in. The nurse and school counselor spoke to other adults at school—keeping Jasmine's name confidential—to ensure that someone spoke to the bullying girls to make sure they didn't do what they'd done to Jasmine to anyone else.

In this way, Jasmine and her therapist used CBT skills to break what otherwise might have been the cycle of racism and racial trauma playing out in Jasmine and her family's life yet again. It's true you might not have a therapist to work through this with the way Jasmine did. But you can use the resources you do have—friends, family members, or trusted adults in your life you can talk to—to understand and apply the skills you've learned in this book to break cycles of trauma-driven behavior. It won't always be easy, and it won't always feel fair to have to carry the burden. But you can learn to be your own advocate, as best you can.

Moving Forward

Grief and feelings of loss are experienced when a person feels they have lost something or won't be able to change something in the ways they may want to. In the next chapter, we will begin exploring how racism and racial trauma can cause you to experience grief.

CHAPTER 7

Understanding Racial Grief and Loss

You cannot change the color of your skin at birth because that is something that is biological. You may begin to feel depressed because you cannot change your skin color to fit in with White peers at school or in your neighborhood. Feeling isolated and alone because of this can lead to feelings of grief (that is, grief that you cannot fit in with your White peers) and loss (that is, feeling that you will lose your friends because of the color of your skin).

Grief is defined as deep sorrow or distress that someone can experience if they encounter a situation that involves sadness or a state of hopelessness. The causes of grief are often dramatic—but they don't have to be. For example, you may have a peer in school make fun of your hair texture, your skin color, or your voice and begin to experience deep sorrow—because you know that Black and mixed-race people have experienced grief for centuries because of slavery, inequality, and discrimination, in part because of judgments people made of their appearance. And you may also experience a sense of grief because it is difficult to believe that anyone would ever act this way, let alone in this day and age—at a time when we're all supposedly equal. Intergenerational trauma that is unresolved or internalized for many years can lead to grief within your family, but you can also experience grief after experiencing anything that you categorize as racism.

Loss is defined as the process of losing something you may consider especially important to you, such as a loved one, a sense of pride in yourself, a sense of ease in your life and your family's life, or even your immediate freedom. For example, you may feel a loss of freedom if you decide you want to live in a certain neighborhood where there are good schools and better opportunities, but because of the color of your skin, you are not accepted in that neighborhood or at that school.

Another example of grief and loss comes from the news media covering violence against Black people. You may experience grief and loss at the news of a Black person being killed by someone who is White. Learning about grief and loss and how you may react to it is important for you to heal racial trauma.

Stages of Grief and Loss

When you experience grief and loss, there are several psychological stages you might go through as you try to come to terms with what you feel. These are denial, anger, depression, bargaining, and acceptance (Gregory 2022). Let's look at them now.

Denial

If you or your family struggle with open communication and talking about the negative impact of racism, you may be experiencing denial—a decision to not acknowledge something that's happening. Because of the negative beliefs that can motivate people to display racist attitudes and behaviors, it may be difficult for you or your family to come to terms with what has happened, so you may refuse to acknowledge that you've experienced racism either personally or as a family. In the end, denial is a protective shield against things that are uncomfortable or painful to talk about. It may be working to make day-to-day life easier to some degree. But it also keeps healing from trauma—when it is overwhelmingly painful—at bay.

What denial may sound like: "Racism does not exist in my life. Everyone accepts me at my school."

Reflection: Can you identify a form of denial in your family? Have you ever been in denial about your race or about racism? If yes, how is that denial helping make what you're dealing with easier? How might it be keeping you from really addressing what you're going through?

Anger

Anger is another emotion that you may experience when facing the truth of your trauma. Anger may be triggered by your own experiences with racism or the experience of others. It's also an understandable response to this racism. After all, we all feel angry when we or the people we love have been wronged and treated badly—especially if it's at the hands of an impersonal system.

But anger is also easy to misdirect, especially when the target of your anger is a system or something outside your direct control. In these cases, you or your family members might find yourselves turning your anger at the people who *are* within the sphere of what you can control—who may not be the ones responsible for the situations that make you angry. Anger that is misdirected in this way can damage your relationships with others. And it can hold you back from healing your trauma. For example, if you are internalizing racism in such a way that you go around being angry with anyone who seems to dislike you, it may be difficult to heal from racial trauma because the anger acts as a defense against deeper emotions that need to be explored and healed. Anger can mask deeper emotions like self-hatred, low self-esteem, and even fear of rejection.

What anger may sound like: "I wish I'd never been born. I hate being me."

Reflection: Can you identify a situation in your life when you directed your anger at the wrong person or thing? How did this anger impact you or others around you?

Depression

As we discussed in chapter 4, depression can cause a lot of emotional and psychological distress. When trauma is difficult to address, it is often easier to internalize the emotions that you have and pretend you are okay. Internalizing emotions and not communicating how you feel can prevent healing from trauma.

What depression may sound like: "I don't want to show my face at school. I'm done with everyone."

Reflection: Can you identify your experience with depression? What did you notice about yourself during this stage?

Bargaining

Sometimes a traumatic experience can cause a state of desperation where you feel the need to give something away or "beg" for something so that you can experience peace of mind again. But that isn't a healthy form of coping with the situation. For example, Jasmine may pray that her bullies transfer to another school and promise that if they do, she will never do another bad thing again. Or she may attempt to give her bullies something in exchange for their friendship. If she does this, she is bargaining so that she can return to a state of normalcy and avoid having to experience the negative thoughts associated with being bullied.

But in the end, bargaining is only a temporary solution to a big problem. And when you bargain, you aren't able to assertively and constructively deal with the grief you're feeling. Bargaining keeps you from being able to address the bigger problems in an unfair situation, including your self-worth and emotional needs.

The opposite of bargaining—and the more useful action in the long run—is acceptance of your situation, assertive action in response to the situation taking the steps you need to in order to take care of yourself, and experiencing personal growth.

What bargaining may sound like: "If I offer something to my bullies—money or favors—they might start to like me."

Reflection: Can you identify some ways that you have tried to bargain so that tough situations you are dealing with would go away—even if temporarily? How have these attempts at bargaining been helpful in the short run? Are there ways they held you back in the long run?

Acceptance

After a traumatic experience, it is normal to experience denial, anger, and depression. It is also normal to bargain or find ways to lessen the grief.

Once you begin to move through the stages of grief and loss in a healthy way, you may begin to feel a sense of calm and relief. Sometimes these feelings are proof that you are beginning to accept what has happened and are able to move forward with your life. In most cases, acceptance of a traumatic experience is a form of growth where you learn how to cope with future experiences a bit better. You also may recognize during this stage that denial and bargaining are unhealthy defenses that will not help you cope with the grief.

What acceptance may sound like: "I shouldn't have to beg for friendship just because I'm Black. I'm okay with who I am, even if they're not."

Reflection: Can you identify some ways that you have accepted the traumatic situation—and feel that it is time to move on in a healthy way?

ACTIVITY 11: STAGES OF LOSS

It is very normal to experience these stages at many points in your life—and you may also experience these stages in a different order. Everyone experiences the stages of grief differently.

How has each of these stages affected you as you heal from racial trauma? You can write down each stage in your journal or use the worksheet you'll find at http://www.newharbinger.com/50126.

Was there ever a time you denied having experienced racism in your life? If the answer is yes, why do you think you denied having experienced racism?

Did you experience anger about the way you were being treated? What did that anger do to you? How did you express anger?

Sometimes depression follows an angry response. Did you experience periods of time where you felt sad or depressed? If yes, why do you think you felt sad or depressed?

Do you think you would ever compromise with someone who is racist just to be accepted by them? If yes, would you bargain by trying to be a nicer person so that you would be accepted?

Do you think you have accepted that racism will continue to exist in the world—even if you do your best to be nice to others and to live peaceably with others? What would acceptance look like to you?

Grief and Secondary Loss

We may grieve when we lose a person who was close to us or someone who represented a major cause that impacts us, such as Dr. Martin Luther King Jr. Sometimes when we are grieving a loss itself, we also experience something known as secondary loss. For example, because of the loss of Dr. Martin Luther King Jr., you are experiencing a loss of self-confidence, a sense of safety, courage, or peace of mind. Or perhaps you have lost the sense of community in your mixed-race neighborhood because of a hate crime against someone who is Black.

ACTIVITY 12: PRIMARY AND SECONDARY LOSS

Below is a list of primary and secondary losses that you may have experienced. At http://www.newharbinger.com/50126, you can download a worksheet with room to write about your experiences.

Sources of primary grief:

• Tragic loss of a Black person discussed on TV or social media

- Racially motivated brutality or crime against a Black person who belongs to your family, your school, or your community

- The death of a family member who supported and encouraged your family to appreciate your roots and heritage

Sources of secondary loss:

- Loss of personal confidence and self-esteem

- Loss of cultural confidence

- Loss of a sense of community because of a hate crime

- Loss of income or educational resources

- Failed friendships and other relationships

- Loss of community supports such as church, school, or work

- Loss of connection to faith or religion

- Feeling of loss of future direction or goals

- Loss of sense of safety

- Loss of trust and respect of authority figures—especially law enforcement or political figures

- Loss of cultural identity because of intergenerational trauma

You may find yourself struggling a lot with primary and secondary loss when you are in the depression and anger stages. When you are feeling depressed, as we discussed in chapter 4, you may begin to think negative thoughts that negatively affect your self-esteem and confidence. Sometimes those negative thoughts are about secondary losses because of the experience of repeated racial trauma.

You may be wondering if your family has gone through the same stages of grief. It is possible that they have. It's also possible that your family experienced something known as the whirlpool of grief. Most Black and mixed-race families who have intergenerational trauma have had this experience.

The Whirlpool of Grief

Let's take a close look at the whirlpool of grief through Jasmine's story.

My family has what is called collective trauma. That means that a group of people have experienced a traumatic event that is relevant to everyone in that group. For example, my family as well as other people in my race have all experienced marginalization that has caused racial trauma. Another example would be that my family has experienced institutionalized racism—making it hard to get employment—just like other people from my race have. My mother told me that Black people have experienced collective trauma for many years because of racism—including social injustice, workplace discrimination, microaggressions, police brutality, and many other things. If this kind of trauma is ignored—as it has been in my family—healing won't take place and my family will continue to suffer from that trauma.

Because of my family's racial trauma my great-grandmother, grandmother, and mother all had PTSD but never spoke about it. They all functioned as if nothing ever really affected them. But it did. My mother recently told me that she felt a deep sadness that she couldn't get rid of. She said that she felt hopeless, confused at times, unloved, and disregarded. She told me that after years of searching for answers—and talking with people who have gone through what she has experienced and made peace with themselves over the trauma—she began to feel calm and stable again. She also took the initiative to learn about her heritage and what her race really meant to her family. She told me that sometimes hearing about other people's stories, exploring history, and embracing our culture through art, music, dance, and other kinds of creative expression helps build confidence and can start the healing process. It was like she finally came through the rainstorm she had been walking in for years. She told me she feels okay now and can move on with her healing. Even though my mom and grandmother wanted to break the cycle of intergenerational trauma when I was born, they just didn't have the skills or supports to change things. That's why I hope to change this negative cycle in our family.

Because the healing process of trauma is so difficult, you may feel yourself getting better one day and feeling stuck the next day. Your emotions may feel like a roller coaster for a while before you finally heal. Dr. Richard Wilson created a model called the whirlpool of grief (Wilson 1992). Originally a lecture handout, this widely published model offers an interesting way to look at your experience of grief and loss and can help you understand the twists and turns of your emotions.

Dr. Wilson explained that grief is a process similar to a whirlpool. There are many rivers, dips, turns, and waterfalls experienced during the grieving period. It isn't always easy to identify what is happening to you but you can certainly feel validated knowing that the grieving process—especially for people who have experienced racial trauma—is a universal experience.

As Dr. Wilson puts it, it's a lot like how an oarsman might feel if he were rowing down the "river of life" when he was suddenly swept over a waterfall and into a whirlpool. A triggering event (for example, an important loss, racial trauma, family trauma, severe bullying) leads to a feeling of being forced down a waterfall; from there, you might experience a series of painful events that feels like being in a whirlpool before you finally find your footing again, find a safe place to anchor yourself so you can exit the whirl-pool, and fully heal from the grief or trauma.

During the "river of life" experience you may feel a variety of emotions such as shock, numbness, and denial. At the bottom of the waterfall, you may feel disorganized and broken. You may experience physical symptoms such as headaches, increased heart rate, nausea, or many of the symptoms discussed in chapter 4. The end of the whirlpool is some form of acceptance and being able to love again or have positive experiences.

ACTIVITY 13: WHIRLPOOL OF GRIEF

In this activity, you will have the chance to reflect upon the many situations involving your race that may have negatively impacted you and your family—and the collective effect these may have had on your sense of well-being and self-worth. Complete the sentences below in your journal or use the worksheet available at http://www. newharbinger.com/50126:

Right now, when I think of the events that have caused me and my family grief, I feel…

My worst memory connected to my grief about the pain of racial trauma is…

This segregation bothers me because…

Sometimes dealing with racism makes me feel…

I always want to be confident but sometimes racism…

The emotions I feel when I think of my race are…

My "river of life" experience has caused me to feel…

Sometimes I feel like my life…

Sometimes I wonder if I am good enough because…

> The emotions I feel when I think about my family's experience with racism, and the experience of racism in my community, are...

You can add anything more you would like to journal about to help yourself explore this activity.

Your experience of racial trauma can feel exactly like the whirlpool of grief—taking you on many twists and turns as you grow as a person. It is okay to feel like your emotions—and maybe your life too—is a whirlpool experience with many valleys and changes ahead. Know that this doesn't mean you can't overcome the challenges. You can.

Figuring Out Who You Are

You may be wondering what you can do to continue growing, changing, and healing in your life after racial trauma. Reflection on your family's history and exploring your own personal meaning and purpose in life can help you continue to grow as a Black or mixed-race person. Building the belief system that you have the power to positively impact your life and make healthy choices for yourself is part of the philosophy known as *existentialism*. This philosophy emphasizes an individual's existence in their own life as a free and responsible person—and a person who has the free will to create themselves and have control over their own choices and actions. Sometimes racism can make you feel powerless and cause you to second-guess yourself. You may find yourself thinking negatively about who you are, including other people of your race. You may also have feelings of confusion around who you are as a person of color as you try to make sense out of the racial trauma you have experienced. You have the capacity for self-reliance and strength, but you may not see that within yourself.

In this section you will be able to reflect upon who you are as a person and who you would like to become on your journey to overcome racial trauma. I have provided examples from my own life to help you reflect on who you really are.

Personal: Growing up in a predominately White neighborhood while being homeschooled was tough when I had to mingle with kids my age who were Black and White. I wasn't White enough to be considered "included" and I wasn't Black enough to mingle with the Black kids. I always had a sense of being excluded and living in two or more different worlds. It wasn't until I entered my midtwenties that I realized there was beauty in my experiences, culture, and ethnicity that made me unique.

Spiritual/religious: Growing up in the Christian faith and not attending church routinely with my family was complicated. The Pentecostal and Baptist faiths have strict rules on church attendance. My mom decided not to enforce church attendance—like she did with my older brother—to help me develop a healthy view of the faith without my feeling pressured. This decision helped me grow spiritually and encouraged me to read the bible, pray, and meditate in an authentic way because I wanted to—not because I needed to.

Social: It took me a long time to appreciate who I was socially. Growing up, I had to embrace the life my mother chose for me, which seemed hard at times. Although I didn't like being rejected in my adolescence by both Black and White people—because of things that set us apart such as being home-school or having friends of various cultures—I came to appreciate the value I added just because of the cultural uniqueness of my experiences over time.

Looking at these three dimensions of myself has helped me see that I am a human being outside of my race. I have other elements to myself that make me who I am.

Now it's your turn.

Personal: A healthy relationship with yourself is important to have—especially when you are healing from racial trauma. You may have a healthy level of self-confidence or like who you are as a person. But sometimes life comes with situations that may cause us to second-guess our identity, strengths, values, and beliefs. When this happens, it may seem impossible to see who we really are. For example, going to school every day to face a group of peers who judge you, say mean things, and seem to enjoy making you feel left out because of your race can cause you to dislike who you are and possibly want to change everything about yourself.

Reflection: Can you think of a time when you wanted to be another race or another person because of racial trauma?

Spiritual/religious: Because of the racial trauma you have experienced, you may feel that life is confusing, unfair, and contradictory. This belief system can cause you to either embrace the idea that there is something bigger than you in the universe that can help you heal from racial trauma (that is, God), or you may feel anger toward spiritual and religious ideas and beliefs. Coping with the experience of unfair and harmful practices against Black and mixed-race people can cause you to lose hope and to lose faith in yourself and in a higher power.

Reflection: Do you believe in a higher power? In what ways can your faith or beliefs help you overcome racial trauma?

Social: Human beings are born to relate to each other and experience the joy that comes with human connection. The experience of racism and racial trauma can cause you to disconnect from other people in your community or school, or peers your age. The fear of rejection as a Black or mixed-race person can cause you to want to hide away from society. But it's important for you to identify your strengths and what you have to offer to the world. Although humans may share some common characteristics, each of us is separate from the other, and we possess individual characteristics that can contribute to the world—your community and other people—in positive ways.

Reflection: Can you think of a time when you contributed to your community or to someone you know in a positive way? How did you feel about that experience?

Visualizing Your Best Self

Now that you have reflected upon the personal, spiritual/religious, and social dimensions of your experience, you can create a visual of your best self, using the steps below. In this activity, I encourage you to write or draw in your journal. I'll start with an example from my own life.

1. I set my timer for five minutes, grab my journal, and begin to draw a picture. My "best self" is confident, happy, and satisfied in my job. In this visualization, I am studying space science. I am sitting at a table on a college campus, and there are books all around me. As I study, I am drinking warm tea and eating a snack. I draw a cup of

tea and a snack. I am envisioning and drawing me putting on a space suit. I am also drawing the helmet over my head.

2. I add some words around my picture such as "brave," "smart," "inspired," and "happy." I also write down words that represents who I want to be in this visualization such as "inspiring to others," "wise," "courageous," "helpful," and "a good example" for Black people interested in space science.

3. When I am done with my picture, I sign my name—Támara Hill— at the top of my page. I then reset my timer to one minute and close my eyes to envision what my life would be like as an astronaut. As I think about putting on the space suit and the helmet, I take three slow deep breaths, and I think about what it would be like to walk around in that space suit. I also allow my mind to explore what the space shuttle would look like. I keep my eyes closed until the timer goes off. When the timer goes off, I take one last deep breath and I open my eyes.

Your turn again.

1. Set a timer for five minutes and draw a picture of your best self. For example, if you aspire to become the president of a big company or you would like to get into the entertainment industry, you could draw a picture of yourself sitting behind a big desk in a big office or draw a picture of yourself performing on stage.

2. If you don't want to draw a picture of yourself, you could draw something that represents what you want to do—like a picture of a dog if you want to become a veterinarian—or you could just write down words that describe who you want to be. For example, if you

aspire to work on your own one day you can write down descriptive words like "business owner," "lawyer," or "artist." Another way to do this activity would be for you to write down what qualities you'd like to see in yourself as you grow older, such as "brave," "happy," or "inspiring."

3. For the final step of this visualization, sign your name at the top of the page, reset your timer for one minute, and then close your eyes and think about the things you wrote down or drew on your page. Make sure you are taking deep breaths as you visualize what you wrote down or drew on your paper. As an alternative to the options above, you could play your favorite music as you complete this activity from start to finish. Music has an interesting influence over the brain, especially a brain dealing with trauma. When music is played during a calming activity, anxiety is reduced because music also decreases blood pressure and improves sleep quality.

Do this once or twice a week as a positive reminder of who you would like to be. Learning to appreciate who you are takes time, patience, and maturity. As you develop over time, you will learn to appreciate who you are if you continue to research your heritage, explore your personal beliefs, embrace new ideas about yourself and your race, and open your heart and mind to the value you bring to life.

Moving Forward

By now, you've learned a lot of tools you can use in your life to help yourself understand and deal with racial trauma and find strength and security in your racial identity and your own unique self. But maybe you're dealing with some problems that call for additional skills beyond these. Or maybe you'd like some help from a professional in implementing the skills and keeping yourself on track in your healing. The next chapter will help you decide whether you should seek additional help and, if so, how to reach out for it.

CHAPTER 8

Reaching Out for Additional Help

For some people it may be helpful to have someone to talk to—someone who isn't in your friend group or your family. Perhaps someone who is trained to listen to you with less judgment and none of their personal opinions—which even our kindest friends or family members sometimes can't help but give us. This person may be your coach, your instructor, a mentor, a neighbor, or a psychotherapist. A child and teen psychotherapist or a trauma therapist can offer a lot of support in your healing of racial trauma.

In this chapter, we'll consider if you're dealing with clinical levels of anxiety, depression, or PTSD, which are all situations for which it can be especially helpful to see a professional (though you don't need to have a diagnosable condition to see a therapist or any other helping professional). Ultimately, it's important to feel comfortable with the person you work with for counseling, and the first step in feeling comfortable is having a psychotherapist who understands how your race influences how you see the world, how you see yourself, and how you exist within your world.

If you do decide to get a psychotherapist at any point, this chapter will help guide you in how to select a good therapist and how therapy with that person might go. We'll also look at some of the roadblocks you or your family might be facing when it comes to working with a professional or navigating the healthcare system, and how you might be able to address those.

Let's begin by considering what the specific symptoms of depression, PTSD, and anxiety are, so you can get the help you need if you're suffering from them.

Learning About Your Symptoms

You are sometimes your own best doctor when you begin to feel unlike yourself. In some cases, you may understand yourself before anyone else can. In other situations, you may feel that you have absolutely no clue what is happening to your mind and your body. Let's look at a few symptoms of depression, anxiety, and PTSD to help you understand what these conditions can look like.

Depression

If you are experiencing depression, you are likely to

feel sad and moody,

feel tired and low-energy most days,

struggle with tearfulness and irritability,

have challenges falling asleep at night or staying asleep,

have a lot of negative thoughts about your self-worth, and

engage in negative self-talk that impacts your self-esteem.

Generally, if you struggle with these symptoms for a period of two weeks or more, you may have depression. You could have something known as situational depression, a kind of depression that shows up only in certain situations and goes away when you are no longer in that situation. For example, you may feel okay most of the time but struggle with situational depression when there is another killing of a Black person on the news. You may recall from chapter 3 that Jasmine tried to avoid seeing her bullies at school because it brought back bad memories of the bullying she experienced. In this case, Jasmine may have situational depression in the morning before school and during the school day.

Of course, symptoms of depression can be tricky to assess because they sometimes look different from what we think depression really is, especially for those of us with racial or family trauma that's never been fully processed. For example, you may feel irritable and cry a lot during the week but never associate these behaviors with depression because they seem so normal to you. You may even hear adults say something like "Teenagers are emotional," which makes it even harder for you to identify that you are depressed.

Reflection: Can you identify any recent or past symptoms you have had that may have been a sign that you were depressed? What did you notice about yourself that was different from how you typically are?

PTSD

If you have PTSD, you may notice symptoms such as

flashbacks or reminders of a traumatic experience you had,

feeling the need to constantly look over your shoulder out of fear of something harming you,

poor concentration and attention span in school or at work, and nightmares or night terrors about a traumatic experience you had.

Sometimes it is hard to identify symptoms of PTSD in everyday life until you begin experiencing repeated nightmares, poor sleep, and flashbacks. These symptoms are often signs that a traumatic experience has caused great distress.

You may have also heard of something known as complex PTSD. Complex PTSD is not a medical diagnosis, but it is something to know about just in case you experience symptoms. Complex PTSD happens when you experience the same traumatic experience over a long period of time—and may not have the proper coping skills to cope with it. For example, if you experience racism in your school for many years—perhaps K through 12—you may begin to experience PTSD symptoms because of the length of time that you experienced racism. You can experience loss of interest in things you once enjoyed, intrusive thoughts about racism that you may have experienced in the past, difficulty with relationships, feelings of hopelessness, feelings of worthlessness, and a negative perception of the world. Although symptoms of complex PTSD may look different from the diagnosis of PTSD, it is still important to know the signs and symptoms so that you can get proper treatment.

Anxiety Disorders

After a traumatic experience, like racism, it is easy to begin experiencing anxiety. Anxiety can manifest itself as

headaches (including migraines),

stomach problems,

muscle tension such as a pinched nerve or stiffness,

nervousness or lack of confidence,

increased heart rate,

racing thoughts, or

sweaty hands and feeling "frozen" or unable to move in a moment of fear.

If things get worse or your anxiety gets out of hand, you may begin to experience panic attacks. Panic attacks are almost always brief moments where anxiety feels so overpowering that you may feel you are losing control of yourself.

Reflection: Can you think of a time when you may have felt like this? What happened and how did you feel?

If any of these symptoms seem like ones you are struggling with, it may be worth it to mention them to someone you trust, perhaps your parent or school counselor, so that you can get support. If you don't take your symptoms seriously and reach out for help, they can get worse.

If you talk to your parents or another adult you trust about experiences like these, you might ultimately decide to try therapy of some kind. Let's take a moment to explore what psychotherapy is and how it works—particularly for those of us who have experienced racial trauma or just want to see a professional who understands our experience.

What Is Psychotherapy?

Psychotherapy is a form of health care that allows you to work with someone you trust to explore your thoughts, feelings, and behaviors. In cases where depression, anxiety, and PTSD are difficult to manage with talk therapy alone, medication may be needed to help the therapy work better. But if you decide not to try medication and to just attend therapy, that's okay too.

There are different kinds of psychotherapy; one that may be helpful to you is *ethnocultural psychotherapy*.

Can you imagine having a psychotherapist who studies the connection between your racial identity and your mental health needs? Psychotherapists Lillian Comas-Diaz and Frederick Jacobsen developed an approach to help psychotherapists better understand clients of color. Ethnocultural psychotherapy seeks to help people fully understand who they are, how their ethnicity and culture influences their lives, and how to manage their strengths in a system that's dominated by unfair political, racial, and socioeconomic power (Comas-Diaz and Jacobsen 1991).

As you have learned in this book, sometimes it can be difficult to identify with your race because of negative feelings or thoughts, so helping you to become aware of your cultural identity and to see it positively is the foundation of this approach. The ethnopsychotherapist may use the therapeutic relationship—your relationship with them—to help you develop more positive thoughts and feelings about your race and identity. This can be very healing.

Another form of psychotherapy that may be helpful is trauma-based CBT psychotherapy. This kind of treatment helps you identify what has caused your trauma, set healthy goals to heal, and learn new ways to cope with trauma. Your CBT trauma therapist would help you explore how much the traumatic experience of racism has impacted you and possibly generations before you. Your parent may have a chance to share some sessions with you as well.

Finding the Right Psychotherapist

Deciding to go to therapy can take some time. You may be feeling a little anxious or sad when you think about going to therapy. Or you may have scheduled an appointment that you aren't sure you are going to keep. Either way, it may be helpful to learn more about the process of seeking therapy, as well as some of the barriers you may face as a Black or mixed-race person and how you might deal with them.

Psychotherapy can be an incredibly positive experience if you find the right therapist who understands you, cares about you, and is able to empathize with you. It can also help you make real and lasting changes if the treatment is appropriate, timely, and meets your needs. If in the end you decide psychotherapy isn't for you—and that you would rather focus on building skills on your own—that's okay too. Psychotherapy isn't for everyone. But if you decide to find a psychotherapist, it is acceptable to look around to find one who is the right fit for you.

Let's look at some common barriers for Black and mixed-race people seeking mental health care.

Barriers to Getting Psychotherapy

If you were to google "how to find a therapist," what do you think will come up? Although you will see various ads and articles giving you tips on how to find a therapist, you will also find that the most popular directories offer the contact information of White psychotherapists more often than Black psychotherapists. To find a Black psychotherapist, you would need to specifically search "how to find a Black therapist" to see a directory at the top of the search results. A statistics research page on zippia.com (2022) shows that about 76.4 percent of therapists are White and only 4.1 percent are Black.

I want you to think about your family for a moment. In some Black and mixed-race families, psychotherapy is feared and demonized because the option to see a Black psychotherapist is often limited. It's sad to think that a shortage of Black psychotherapists on Google would make it hard for you to consider going to psychotherapy.

I once provided psychotherapy to a mixed-race couple dealing with racial trauma. They told me they held a negative view of treatment because they did not want to get help from a person who didn't look like them, may not understand them, and who once oppressed an entire group of people.

Certain racial groups—especially the Black, Native American, and Hispanic cultures—avoid, or have limited access to, psychotherapy. They may struggle with a fear of being judged, unfairly labeled, stigmatized as "crazy," or seen as a "project." This can be a major barrier to getting proper treatment and reaching out for help.

In the activity below, you will be able to explore some of your own barriers to getting psychotherapy.

ACTIVITY 14: BARRIERS YOU MAY FACE

This activity allows you to identify the barriers you feel you may be up against in trying to get psychotherapy. Whether these barriers are financial, logistical (for example, transportation challenges), or related to your race, culture, or family perceptions, it can be helpful to make note of them and examine if you can work around them.

You can use your journal or the worksheet online at http://www.newharbinger.com/50126 to assist you identifying these barriers.

Financial Barriers

- Not having enough money to spend on psychotherapy

- Not having insurance or not being able to find the right psychotherapist who accepts your insurance

- Parent(s) divorcing/separating, and insurance is changing or ending soon

Solution to Financial Barriers

There are organizations that may help you with financial assistance to see a therapist. An organization at lovelandfoundation.org helps BIPOC communities find affordable therapy.

If you find a therapist that you like, you can ask them if your mom or dad can pay a flat fee (for example, $50 a session) or a sliding fee (for example, $50–$80 a session). Sliding scale fees may change depending on how much therapy you need but it is often a good way to get treatment at a lower cost.

Cultural Barriers

- Incorrect views of mental health problems and what mental health care is

- Fear of being judged, stigmatized, or incorrectly diagnosed/labeled with a mental health condition

- Having a single parent household and facing challenges around getting to the psychotherapist on time, being able to see the psychotherapist alone without siblings or the parent in the waiting area or having to cancel the appointment because the parent has no childcare

- Premature termination of treatment (for example, dropping out of counseling or refusing to return)

- Acculturation process (People who are not fully acculturated may find it difficult to trust psychotherapists who do not look or sound like them.)

Solution to Cultural Barriers

There are some directories that list psychotherapists who are part of BIPOC communities; for examples Therapy for Black Girls (therapyforblackgirls.com) and Therapy for Black Men (therapyforblackmen.org).

Geographical Barriers

- Lack of access to transit services or transportation

- Lack of consistent transportation

- Living in a rural (country) area or inner city where transportation services are scarce or really expensive

Solution to Geographical Barriers

Look up teletherapy online or ask your local doctor's office for a list of psychotherapists who offer teletherapy.

Now that we have looked at some of the barriers to getting psychotherapy, let's look at Jasmine's experience in trying to make her first appointment.

I made the call for my first therapy appointment with my grandmother. Because this was new to me, I asked her to help me find someone good. My grandmother didn't always seem comfortable getting on the phone with the people we talked to—I don't think we're a family big on therapy. But she told me that she cared about me and wanted to get me help, so we'd do it together. She called a few places and left our phone number. Some therapists called us back and some did not.

One lady called and said she didn't accept our insurance. She told my grandmother that we would have to pay her rate, which was $120 *per hour. That was a lot of money. My grandmother told her we would have to keep searching.*

Then Grandma looked at me and asked me if I wanted to speak to the next therapist we would call. I felt a little nervous, but I took a mindful breath or two and then went for it. A nice lady picked up the phone and said, "Welcome to Caring Place! How may I help you today?" I told her that I was fourteen years old and needed to talk to someone. I told her I was new to all of this and didn't know what to say or what to expect. She was so nice, and she told me she could start by doing a video session with me and my grandmother together after school tomorrow and explain everything to us. I was so happy that she seemed "normal." She didn't judge me. She didn't talk to me like I was a kid. She was great!

I asked what I would need to do to prepare for tomorrow, and she told me nothing at all. She also told me that they do take my insurance and that my grandmother would only have to pay a small amount each session. My grandma asked her if there were therapists there who could help me with racial bullying. She told my grandma that she is mixed-race and that the boss of the place is also mixed-race. She told me I could go online to their website and read about the therapists who work there if I wanted to know more. They were all mixed-race and had experience with racism. I was glad to hear that I wasn't getting any kind of therapist who couldn't understand me. And I was thrilled for the video session the next day.

Have you ever had an experience like Jasmine's? If not, perhaps you will if you decide therapy is for you. Some people have had therapists in the past and found that things didn't go so well. Other people may have had positive experiences. It just depends on who you see, why you are seeing them, and if they can relate to you in any way.

If you decide that you want someone who specializes in treating people who have experienced racism, seeing a psychotherapist who understands cultural oppression (that is, racism, prejudice, and discrimination) might be the best road to take.

Other Paths to Explore

If you struggle with finances or do not know where to look for a good therapist in your area, you can certainly reach out for support in other ways. One good alternative is your school counselor. School counselors can help you explore the thoughts and feelings you may be experiencing during the school day. They can also offer free resources in case of an emergency, such as a crisis hotline or a mental health text service. A school counselor is also able to speak on your behalf if you need academic supports—such as a 504 plan or an individualized education plan (IEP)— to help you when you are depressed or anxious. You may be wondering if you will have privacy and confidentiality with a school counselor. The answer is that this really depends on the school, but legally—and ethically—you are entitled to privacy and confidentiality unless you are a danger to yourself and/or others or you are being abused. School counselors can truly support you in the event you aren't able to see a private psychotherapist.

Let's examine one last option that may help you if you decide seeing a therapist isn't for you.

Healing Grief Through Community

Research in the field of psychology tells us that we can disarm racism, discrimination, and racial trauma with *microinterventions* (Sue 2021). Microinterventions are antibias ways that we can behave everyday within a community to help us counteract racism and discrimination. For example, if you counteract racism and bias with confidence when you experience or see it, that would be regarded as a microintervention.

Sometimes taking care of yourself means standing up for what is right and finding people within your community who know just how to do this. Your mentors, coaches, instructors, advisors, teachers, neighbors, and other well-meaning adults can contribute to your community in positive ways and support Black and mixed-race people by donating, painting murals in the neighborhood, picking up trash and litter, volunteering, babysitting or providing childcare, offering tutoring, and more. You may find a mentor at your school and at the local library or social club who may be willing to offer you support and guidance.

You can also contribute to your community in positive ways. You can do small things in your daily life—or whenever an opportunity presents itself—to support and uplift your community and empower yourself at the same time. You can lead by example. Some groups to consider learning more about include the Color of Change (Colorofchange.org), NAACP.org (National Association for the Advancement of Colored People), or Black Girls Code (blackgirlscode.com). Each of these organizations work with the community to support Black and mixed-race people in the nation. Joining one of these groups would be a microintervention in and of itself.

Healing from trauma may seem like an overwhelming process—especially because of the feelings of loss and grief that you may have to work through. Feeling like you have lost something important to you—your confidence, your ability to feel safe in your school and community, or your friendships—can be really hard to accept. But thankfully there are healthy ways to overcome that feeling of grief and loss and contribute to your community in healthy ways.

Moving Forward

Sometimes it is very healing to label our experiences for what they truly are rather than pretending they don't exist. No matter how painful racism is, facing the situation and how you feel, growing from the experience, and healing by doing some of the things suggested in this book can be helpful. Whether or not you decide to seek additional help, with the new skills you have learned, you are in a better position to cope in healthy ways with any future experiences of racism and break generational trauma in your family.

It is so important to stay connected to the positive roots of your heritage and have someone to talk to about your thoughts and feelings. Hold tightly to the values you hold and the positive role models you have, and prioritize your mental health so that you will be able to accomplish your short- and long-term goals.

CHAPTER 9

Moving into Your Future

We have covered quite a few things in this book. We looked at the development of negative thought patterns after being exposed to racial trauma and racism. We learned how negative thoughts and beliefs—which are often rooted in intergenerational trauma—can cause us to believe things about ourselves that isn't true. Microaggressions, covert and overt racism, familial trauma, and the resulting cognitive distortions often cause Black and mixed-race people to feel rejected and unwanted in society. These deep-seated beliefs can lead to PTSD, depression, and anxiety, and you may also notice your general sense of self-esteem, confidence, and self-worth decrease as you encounter racism in specific places like school or work or in the broader community.

Thankfully, there are ways to heal from racial trauma that include acknowledging that you are experiencing racism in your life and learning how to openly communicate how you are feeling as you heal. You can and have engaged in positive activities while reading this book, such as journaling, creating a safety and wellness plan, possibly finding a psychotherapist you like, and engaging in self-empowerment activities within your community.

I hope you have learned a bit more about yourself, your race, and the ways that you think, feel, and behave in response to racism. Healing from racial trauma takes time, time to find the right answers and the keys to the negative thoughts and emotions you may have locked away. But once you find the tools that work best for you, you can begin the healing process. That process may include specific tools, and it may include a variety of tools. Your healing is up to you.

You've also been able to learn a bit about my own experience dealing with racism and racial trauma. There are a lot of things that weigh on my heart as a human, Black and mixed-race woman, and psychotherapist—but one of the most burdensome areas of study for me is racism. It's often very hard for me to understand how to be a light in a world that seems very unfair and constructed in the favor of White descendants. When I experience equal and caring relationships with my White colleagues, family, and friends, I feel hopeful. And I hope through some of your experiences with caring White peers, teachers, bosses, and others that you feel hopeful too.

What we learn about ourselves and others through a little exploration can always surprise us. It surprised me many times over the course of my life as a Black and mixed-race person. Learning about yourself and how you respond to racism can also cause a lot of grief and feelings of loss, in addition to the discovery of your own power and capacity for resilience. But as you have learned, grieving is a normal process—especially if you have felt mistreated, discriminated against, and misunderstood, and if your family has suffered due to racism and other forms of trauma. And grieving doesn't have to be the end of your story. You can learn to understand the thoughts and feelings you have, and learn how to deal with them. You can turn to the helpful and supportive people in your life for help with what you're dealing with, and be of help to them in turn. You can work with your family and friends to understand the society we live in, and work to change it. Ultimately, you can take the grief that racism may have caused you and turn it into a learning experience, a source of strength that will carry you for the rest of your life.

As you continue your life as a Black or mixed-race person, I hope you remember that understanding and coping with racial trauma is a lifelong journey—a journey that may seem difficult at first but can build strength within you as you learn more about who you are, who your family is, and how racial trauma impacts your community. For as long as racism is going to be both an individual and a systemic issue, you are likely to continue to encounter it—but you don't have to accept it and you don't have to remain discouraged by it. With the right mindset and the right tools, you have the power to change how you react to racism and how you react to the racism that has affected your family.

Even though it may seem like some forms of racism have decreased in our society, we are far from eradicating racism in our community, which means that you must continue to fully understand your personal and family worth so that racism can no longer have power over your identity, self-esteem, and confidence. One of the most powerful mind games of racism is to cause you to believe that you are not worthy—that you are not valuable in the community. Defeating that cognitive distortion is the first step toward healing.

Ongoing experiences of racism do not occur because of who you are—they occur because of systemic oppression and historical disparities and differences in access to financial stability, good schools and neighborhoods, and other necessities for living. But you have the power to change your life and evolve in positive ways—you just have to believe that.

I hope this book has encouraged you to discover your true identity and appreciate all that you are—and all that you are becoming as you heal from racial trauma.

Acknowledgments

To my mother, Sabrina Hill: Thank you for raising me and taking me down a cultural and self-taught path that enlightened me to know exactly who I am and to the One who made me.

To my brother Ryan Hill, for helping me along the way with your technical knowledge and unfathomable insights.

To my older brother, Shamar Hill: Here's the book we have always needed to validate so many cultural experiences we were never fully prepared for.

To my clients/patients for helping me grow by sharing with me the sensitivities of your stories. You have had a part in making me the clinician I am today.

To New Harbinger Publications: Thank you for giving me this opportunity to contribute to the world on such an important topic. I'm grateful to have worked with and learned from Jennye and Vicraj.

To Joshua McKivigan, LPC; Donald Laird, LPC; and Dr. Taunya Tinsley, PhD: Thank you for your work in this field and for your contribution to this important work that is close to my heart.

To Dr. Earl Turner, PhD: Thank you so much for your contribution and writing an impactful foreword.

To Kaii Marie: Thank you for your support and for leading the Black community in holistic health.

To Lori Maldonado: Thank you for always supporting and offering me opportunities in the educational and academic world.

To Anat Samid: Thank you for participating in this and for the work that you do!

I believe it takes a village to raise a child—and a village to build one person up. Thank you.

References

Comas-Díaz, L., and F. M. Jacobsen (1991). "Ethnocultural Transference and Countertransference in the Therapeutic Dyad." *American Journal of Orthopsychiatry* 61(3), 392–402.

Gregory, C. "The Five Stages of Grief: An Examination of the Kubler-Ross Model." Psycom. Last updated June 7, 2022. https://www.psycom.net /depression.central.grief.html.

National Museum of African American History & Culture. "Race and Racial Identity." Accessed April 17, 2022. https://nmaahc.si.edu/learn /talking-about-race/topics/race-and-racial-identity.

Scientific American. 2021. "When Good People Must Act: In Scientific American, Derald Wing Sue makes the case for 'microinterventions.'" https://www.tc.columbia.edu/articles/2021/april/in-scientific-american -derald-wing-sue-makes-the-case-for-microinterventions/.

Sue D. W., C. M. Capodilupo, G. C. Torino, J. M. Bucceri, A. M. Holder, K. L. Nadal, and M. Esquilin. 2007. "Racial Microaggressions in Everyday Life: Implications for Clinical Practice." *American Psychologist* 62(4): 271–86.

Wilson R. 1992. The Whirlpool of Grief. Lecture handout from Child and Death International Conference, Edinburgh.

Zippia: The Career Expert. 2022. "Therapist Demographics and Statistics in the US." https://www.zippia.com/therapist-jobs/demographics/.

Támara Hill, LPC, is a licensed clinical child and family therapist, and an internationally/board-certified trauma therapist who specializes in treating children, adolescents, and families who suffer from mood disorders, unresolved trauma, and disruptive behavioral disorders. She also provides international consultations and works with young and older adults struggling with grief and loss or life transitions. Hill strives to help clients to realize and actualize their strengths in their home environments and in their relationships within the community. She is internationally recognized for corresponding literary works, as well as appearances on radio and other media platforms. She is an international and keynote speaker, family consultant, and founder of Anchored Child & Family Counseling in Pittsburgh, PA.

Foreword writer **Erlanger A. Turner, PhD**, is a clinical psychologist, and assistant professor of psychology at Pepperdine University in Los Angeles, CA. Turner is a member of the American Psychological Association and The Association of Black Psychologists. He is also past president of the Society for Child and Family Policy and Practice, and served on the board of directors for the Society of Clinical Child and Adolescent Psychology. Recently, Turner founded Therapy for Black Kids to help promote resilience and healthy emotional development. Finally, Turner is a member of the advisory board for the *Sesame Street* racial justice initiative. You can find out more about Turner at www.drerlangerturner.com.

MORE BOOKS from
NEW HARBINGER PUBLICATIONS

Did you know there are **free tools** you can download for this book?

Free tools are things like **worksheets, guided meditation exercises**, and **more** that will help you get the most out of your book.

You can download free tools for this book—whether you bought or borrowed it, in any format, from any source—from the New Harbinger website. All you need is a NewHarbinger.com account. Just use the URL provided in this book to view the free tools that are available for it. Then, click on the "download" button for the free tool you want, and follow the prompts that appear to log in to your NewHarbinger.com account and download the material.

You can also save the free tools for this book to your **Free Tools Library** so you can access them again anytime, just by logging in to your account! Just look for this button on the book's free tools page.

+ Save this to my free tools library